# Ask the

# cat Keeper

## MARC MORRONE
with Amy Fernandez

Original Illustrations © 2009 by Jason O'Malley. Photographs © 2009 by Tara Darling and Isabelle Français.

Library of Congress Cataloging-in-Publication Data

Morrone, Marc, 1960-
  [Ask the cat keeper]
  Marc Morrone's ask the cat keeper / by Marc Morrone with Amy Fernandez.
     p. cm.
  ISBN 978-1-933958-30-9
  1. Cats—Miscellanea. 2. Cats—Health—Miscellanea. 3. Cats—Behavior—Miscellanea. I. Fernandez, Amy. II. Title. III. Title: Ask the cat keeper.
  SF447.M69 2009
  636.8—dc22
                                        2009009827


BowTie Press®
A Division of BowTie, Inc.
3 Burroughs
Irvine, California, 92618

Printed and bound in Singapore
16 15 14 13 12 11 10 09        1 2 3 4 5 6 7 8 9 10

# CONTENTS

To Rocky,
who was a teeny-weeny little cat yet
brought a great deal of comfort to me
in a dark time of my life.

# FOREWORD

BY MARTHA STEWART

I was a cat lover before I loved dogs.

At a country fair in Woodstock, New York, someone had a basket of longhair cats, and I chose the darkest kitty with the longest hair and named it Chigi after one of the Italian popes. Never having owned a cat before, I took it home to our big apartment on Riverside Drive in New York City, where it quickly ingratiated itself into our lives. It was playful, it fetched and returned little stuffed toys, and it answered the telephone each time it rang, knocking the receiver off the hook and meowing a big hello to anyone on the line.

Chigi died at about five from cancer, but I quickly adopted another longhair that was also part Persian.

Chigi II was also a phenomenal cat, and she made the move with us to Westport, Connecticut, and made her home with us at Turkey Hill, wandering in and out of the house, traveling in our car wherever we traveled. She loved to hunt and loved to please, and she loved fresh raw beef kidney chopped into small pieces.

After the two Chigis, I discovered Persians and then Himalayans. I found that I really got along very well with the flattish-faced, longhair, colorful, fluffy, and gently friendly breeds that loved attention but did not demand it, respected the furniture, and coexisted nicely with the dogs, family, and friends. I started with one and kept adding until at one time we housed nine cats at Turkey Hill in Westport. If cats are well groomed, cared for sensibly by the veterinarian, and fed very well, they can live for more than twenty years. All of the beauties that are with me now are over twelve except for the newest addition, Sir Frost, who was adopted at ten, and all go outside every day, eat well, and sleep in baskets, on cushions, and on chairs or beds all over the house. Each also answers to its name and comes (usually) when called. I personally comb and groom them once a week on Sunday, but they are also groomed during the week by others. Ears are cleaned and teeth checked for tartar buildup, and gums are checked for problems.

Cats are so very less demanding of attention than dogs are, but they crave petting, conversation, and love despite their more aloof attitudes. The excellent advice Marc Morrone gives in this book will help anyone with cats enjoy pet ownership even more. And possibly you will add more cats to your life, as I have done, keeping vitality and charm and interest in your household.

## All of the Cats I Have Owned:

Chigi Toto—adopted in Woodstock, NY
Chigi Toto II—adopted from Bide-a-Wee home
New kitty—adopted from Molly Vogel
China cat—adopted from Florida
Uncle Vanya—blue Persian, ASPCA
Uncle Vanya II—blue Persian, ASPCA
Magnolia—silver Persian, adopted
Teeny—blue point Himalayan, adopted
Weeny—lavender point Himalayan, adopted
Mozart—lynx Himalayan, aged 18
Beethoven—flame point Himalayan
Bartok—seal point Himalayan, aged 17
Berlioz—flame point Himalayan
Verdi—Himalayan, aged 12
Vivaldi—Himalayan, aged 12
Elektra—lynx Himalayan, given away
Sirius—lynx Himalayan
Sir Frost—blue point Himalayan, adopted, aged 10
Lady Snow—Himalayan, adopted but returned

# INTRODUCTION

The cat is the pet of contrast. Consider that the words *dog* and *domesticated* both begin with the letter *d*; the dog is the most domesticated animal in the world. The late, great Roger Caras defined the dog as a species whose genes are controlled by man. However, the words *cat* and *contrast* both begin with the letter *c*, and a cat is definitely a contrast between a wild and a domesticated animal. The cat is the only domesticated animal that voluntarily chooses this state. In the course of an hour, a cat can change from a pampered pet dozing contentedly on a fluffy pillow in the living room to a steely-eyed killer crouching in the underbrush, stalking small birds and rodents. Then, just as quickly, he can walk back into the role of pampered pet. No other domesticated animal can do this. Some, such as goats and pigs, can choose to live in a feral state, but once they are totally feral they will never revert to a domesticated state. Only the cat can live in both worlds. If the human race vanished, so would dogs. Cats would continue as long as there were mice to catch—and there will always be mice!

Human opinions toward cats are another outstanding source of contrast. Some humans value cats as family members. At the same time, cats are hated and vilified by others. To this day, some of my own relatives believe that a cat will suck a baby's breath away. Throughout history, cats have experienced treatment ranging from deification by the ancient Egyptians to being burned alive as agents of Satan by Medieval Europeans. And the cats themselves never did anything to specifically attract adulation or persecution; they have simply been cats.

Perhaps because it is generally believed that cats have not been domesticated as long as dogs have (less than 10,000 years), we have not yet come to understand what a cat truly is. The domesticated cat has changed very little from its wild ancestor, the North African wild cat—there are perhaps only small variations in size, coat length, color, and ear shape. The only taxonomic variation is that the domestic cat comes into heat two or three times a year, whereas the North African wild cat comes into heat once a year. The biggest difference between wild and domestic cats is in their behavior. When a wild cat reaches adolescence, the family unit breaks up and each cat lives independently as an adult; individuals interact only during mating season. In contrast, adult domestic cats voluntarily seek attention from not only humans but also other species in the household. The interesting thing is that cats do this by choice. Dogs are genetically programmed to respond this way, thanks to thousands of years of selective breeding. The same cannot be said for cats. Humans kept cats around because they were useful to help control rats and mice, but historically no one made any effort to selectively instill particular temperament traits in the cat.

Another contrast is the way that our society is divided into cat lovers and dog lovers. Dog lovers disparage cats as being too aloof and independent. But in reality, cats love humans in a much more realistic way than dogs do. Cats do this of their own free will. In my opinion, this is one of the unique characteristics of pet cats. Unfortunately, the cat hides many secrets. It can be hard for us to understand much of what they do, especially when it conflicts with our own lifestyles. This causes many problems in human-cat relationships. If we just try to look at the world through a cat's green, gold, copper, or blue eyes, we can better understand their behavior and how we can work to make our cats complement, rather than complicate, our lives.

## Kitty and the Cat Chow

Commercial cat food really wasn't widely available until fairly recently (twentieth century). Before that, the majority of house cats received a bowl of milk in the morning and evening and basically had to fend for themselves otherwise. Ardent cat lovers at that time, who were definitely in the minority, went to the butcher to get meat scraps for their cats. Cats could not survive on the same kind of "people-food" leftovers that were given to pet dogs.

One thing we need to realize is that cats are obligate carnivores—they need to eat meat. Whether you feed your cat canned food or dry food, be sure that the first ingredients listed on the label are pure meat. Cats don't see colors as we do, so there is no point in buying cat food containing little orange pieces of cheese or little green fish. Those things are put into the food strictly for our benefit. Your cat couldn't care less if the food is colorful or makes its own special gravy. Manufacturers may include these things in foods just so they will appeal to the cat owners who buy them.

The first cat I owned, when I was six years old, was a black kitten named Kitty. Back in those days, the only commercial cat food was good old Purina Cat Chow. It was made in little star shapes. I remember wondering aloud why the cat food was shaped like stars. My father informed me that less food would fit in the box this way, so the cat food company would make more money. But I remember intently watching my cat eat these little star-shaped pieces of food. He would nip off the tips of each star with his back teeth. Apparently, this shape made it easier for cats to eat the food. Obviously, there was a very good reason for making cat food in this shape. Somebody somewhere had made this discovery by closely observing the way cats eat. They knew that cats preferred this star shape over all others. That's when I came to the realization that there were people out there who were equally fascinated with pet keeping. Knowing this made me feel better, because my family and friends thought I was nuts for sitting on the floor with my head on my hands, watching the cat eat. I also noticed that the cat seemed to prefer eating the food dry rather than soaked in milk; the latter is what many people believed. This was when I started doing my own research on pet keeping rather than accepting advice at face value.

Many people are quite emotional regarding the best foods for cats and the best ways to feed them. It's a very hot topic, and I refuse to tell you what to do. I can only share my experiences. My cats have always done the best on a raw diet. However, preparing a raw diet is quite expensive, and you must ensure that it is nutritionally balanced. It is easier to buy a prepared frozen raw diet, which can be found in many pet shops. But they also tend to be quite expensive, especially if you have multiple cats, as I do. So I have found that a premium-quality canned food is the best compromise. If you want to take advantage of my advice, it is based on my experience rather than on something I have read or seen on the Internet. And I am certainly not charging for my services—nor will I judge you for not accepting my advice if it does not fit your lifestyle.

Cats are extremely adaptable animals. They have traveled with us all over the globe, eating all sorts of foods. If your cat is doing just fine on a dry kibble diet that you buy in 50-pound bags at a big discount retailer, that's fine; don't worry about it. But it doesn't work for every cat. You might want to try different diets and see for yourself what is best for your cat. As a responsible pet keeper, you should always be looking for new, different, and better ways to maintain your pets.

## Are raw diets really better for cats?

I never paid much attention to diets for cats until my favorite cat, Rocky, a tortie-point Siamese, developed horrible skin allergies. This was before the days when raw diets were popular. My vet gave him cortisone injections to temporarily relieve the symptoms. I thought that processed cat food might be contributing to his problem, as the cats of my youth never had these issues, so I decided to try introducing him to a totally natural diet. Since our freezer was always full of frozen mice and rats to feed our reptiles and birds of prey, I thawed out a few, put them on a plate, and offered them to Rocky. The cats of my childhood always loved mice and rats. However, when Rocky was presented with a dish of mice, he looked at me in abject horror. I wasn't about to mince the mice to try to convince him to eat them, so I went on to plan B. I mixed raw ground chicken, turkey, and beef, added some vitamin calcium supplement that I give to my reptiles, added a bit of steamed mashed vegetables, and gave

that to Rocky. Again, Rocky was horrified. So I lightly cooked this mixture in the microwave and then he ate it. Little by little, I cooked it less, and he finally accepted eating it raw. Literally, within two weeks of eating this raw diet, his skin problems cleared up. But then, of course, all of my other cats wanted to eat the same food, and it became very time consuming and expensive. I did a little research and found companies that made frozen raw diets that could be shipped, packed in dry ice. But this was also extremely expensive. So once Rocky had been doing well on the raw diet for six or seven months, I gradually switched him to a premium-quality canned food. Apparently, eating the raw diet for a few months had fixed whatever wiring was loose in his system, and for the rest of his life he did fine on this canned food. Pet keeping is full of experimentation, common sense, and seeing every animal as an individual.

## Should I feed my cat wet or dry food? Does it matter?

When I was a kid, all of our cats ate dry food and stayed outside all day long eating birds, mice, and lizards. However, one thing I've noticed is that now that I keep cats indoors and they are fed a diet of dry food, they tend to be much

heavier, shed a lot more, and throw up a lot more. In the vomit, I notice that a lot of the dry food is not well chewed. Cats just swallow it whole or crack it in half with their back teeth. Their teeth are really not designed for chewing dry food like dogs do. Some cats chew dry food better than with others do, and the carbohydrates in dry food agree with some cats better than with others.

When I switched my cats to canned food, the vomiting stopped immediately. The shedding decreased, they lost weight, and their general attitude improved. These changes are even more pronounced when cats are put on a raw food diet, but, as I mentioned, that was too expensive and time consuming. I am quite satisfied with how they do on canned food. If you feed your cats dry food and want to find out if they would do better on canned, switch for a few weeks. If you are satisfied with the results, you won't go back to dry food. But you may not notice a change; every cat is different. Good pet keeping involves trying new and different ideas; it never hurts to try something new if you have the option.

### Is it better to feed my cat at certain times of the day? What if he gets hungry while I am at work? Should I leave a dish of dry cat food out for him to snack on?

I used to give my cats some canned food in the morning and in the evening. I would also leave dry food out for them during the day. But I found that my cats were eating the dry food all day long and consequently becoming way too fat!

I started giving them as much canned food as they could eat twice a day, with nothing in between. They always act like they are starving by meal time, but they seem to be much healthier. They have lost weight and they shed less on this dietary regime. This feeding schedule is actually more natural for cats. In a state of nature, a cat would not have the opportunity to nosh all day long. He would hunt, catch prey, eat it, and go to sleep for a while. When he awoke hungry, the whole process would start again.

Grazing all day long is really not a natural way for cats to eat. Of course, this is just my opinion based on my experiences with feeding my own cats. Many people do let their cats nosh on dry food all day, and these cats do fine. So you as the pet keeper must decide what is best for your cat.

## One of my cats is overweight; how can I put him on a diet while letting my other cats eat regular meals?

The best thing to do is to stop feeding dry food. Feed the cats only canned food. This way it's not an issue to put a dish of food in front of each cat at mealtime. When they are finished, you know exactly how much each one has eaten. Pick up any remaining food as soon as each cat is done. If the overweight cat finishes eating first, pick him up so he cannot eat the other cats' food.

It is impossible to do this when feeding dry food because cats don't eat it fast enough. Cats on a diet of canned food will naturally lose weight anyway because they no longer have the option of grazing all day, which is an unnatural situation for a carnivore.

## Are vegetable-formula cat foods really healthy, or is it all a bunch of hype?

Although dogs can do well on a carefully prepared vegetarian diet, cats are obligate carnivores. There is no way a cat can do well on a vegan diet, although some diehard vegans will argue with this. Cats need taurine, which is found only in animal protein. Without it, the cat will go blind, die, or both. There are synthetic sources of protein, and some vegans have tried adding this to a soybean-type cat diet. Technically, this might keep the cat alive, but I think it is wrong to force your beliefs down your pet's throat. If you are a devout vegan and you want to keep a pet, get a rabbit or a guinea pig, which will appreciate your dietary regime.

## Is it OK for my cat to eat grass? Why do cats like it so much?

Cats are obligate carnivores and cannot digest grass at all. Cats will eat it because they love its taste and texture. When a cat does eat grass, he will throw it up a few hours later because he cannot digest it. Many people assume that cats eat grass to make themselves throw up, but there is no way a cat has that level of cognitive function. He eats it merely because he likes it and throws it up merely because he can't digest it.

## Should I buy potted grass for my cat? Does he need this? Is it good for him? Will it prevent hairballs?

Many cats enjoy eating grass and other vegetation, but this isn't because their bodies tell them that they need it. They like to chew on grass because they like the way it feels in their mouths. This is also why some cats chew on wool, paper, or plastic.

When a cat eats grass or a spider plant—which is actually poisonous to him—he cannot digest it. If he eats a small amount of a Boston fern or kitty greens, it will be passed through his intestines. If he eats a large amount, it won't be able to pass through him that way, and he will throw it up. Cats' stomachs always contain some hair because of their constant grooming. If he happens to eat a large quantity of grass and then vomits it up, it will inevitably be mixed with some hair. This can make you think that the cat ate the grass in an effort to get rid of a hairball, but this is just a coincidence.

Kitty greens are very soft three-day-old rye grass, which is much less likely to irritate the cat's digestive tract. If your cat enjoys kitty greens and he does not consume so much that he experiences digestive problems, it's fine to give them to him.

I have one young adult cat and one senior cat; is there one food I can give to both of them or does my older cat need a "senior formula"?

People may argue with me, but as a general rule, all of my cats eat the same thing. We have eight cats, varying in age from eight weeks to eighteen years, and it is impossible to keep them all separated. They get a good-quality canned food, and they all do fine. This is the only way I can do it in my house.

I've read that milk is unhealthy for cats, but my family has always given our cats a saucer of milk as a special treat. Are some cats OK with it?

Milk isn't bad for cats, and most enjoy it. But they don't have the enzymes to digest it properly, which can result in soft stools. Farmers always fed their cats milk in the morning, but these barn cats were also out eating birds and rodents. Fur and feathers probably helped counteract the problem. And they lived in the barn, not the house, so loose stools were not an issue.

A little milk won't hurt the cat, but a whole saucer might be overdoing it. Use your own judgment. If your cat is doing fine and you have no trouble keeping his litter box clean, let him have it.

My cat seems to love ice cream and yogurt and won't leave me alone whenever I'm eating either. Is it OK to let him have the occasional taste?

A little of these foods won't hurt the cat. But if he is eating so much that he has trouble digesting it or has no appetite for his cat food, it's going to cause problems. Chocolate is harmful to both cats and dogs, so it's best not to allow your pet to have chocolate ice cream.

Why does my cat drink so much less water than my dog does?

The North African wild cat, the ancestor of the domestic cat, was a desert animal. As such, cats

evolved to need very little water in order to survive. Their diet consisted almost exclusively of live game, and their prey's body fluids also provided a source of water. The wild cats didn't need to actually drink much. But cats that live as domesticated indoor pets don't have the opportunity to eat live prey, so they need to drink water. This is contrary to their wild instinct. However, if the cat doesn't drink enough water, it can cause problems. The cat will live in a constant state of dehydration, and this can cause compromised kidney function.

## Should I add fruits and vegetables to my cat's diet?

Some cats will eat fruits such as bananas and blueberries. However, cats are obligate carnivores. In nature, cats would not consume grains or fruits other than what they found in the digestive tracts of their prey. If your cat likes the taste of fruit, an occasional treat won't hurt him. But if he doesn't like it, don't worry.

## Is dry food good for my cat's teeth? Will eating dry food keep his teeth clean?

The idea that dry food will keep any animal's teeth clean is akin to thinking that eating a bowl of dry Cheerios will keep your teeth clean. The only way to keep his teeth clean is to go in there with a toothbrush and toothpaste and brush them as often as you can. Once a year, have a tooth cleaning done professionally by your veterinarian.

In nature, if a cat eats a bird or a mouse, the feathers or fur acts as dental floss to keep his teeth clean. Feathers and fur in his digestive tract also sweep it clean. Dry cat food won't do the same thing.

### BASH THE ASH

Any processed food contains some ash. Some cats, particularly males, don't do well with too much ash in their diet. Cat food manufacturers now know this, and cat food formulas contain the minimal amount as set forth by the Association of American Feed Control Officials (AAFCO). But more highly processed foods contain more ash, and dry cat foods have more than canned.

## What are the best treats for my cat, and how often should I give them to her?

I can't imagine why a cat would need treats. My cats have a great life as it is, but I don't judge people who want to give their cats a little something extra. Cat food is so tasty and full of meat, and there is very little that cats like better. But the best treats for cats are bits of meat. Some cats do like meats with salt, sugar, and fat, like deli meats. A little of this won't hurt them, but don't overdo it. Chicken and turkey baby food is a cat favorite. Most trainers use these as training rewards.

## Should Persian cats be fed out of elevated dishes?

I've owned Persian cats all my life, and I've never fed them from raised dishes. They have short legs, so how tall can you make the dish? One thing I have noticed is that most cats prefer to drink from tall glasses rather than flat dishes on the floor. If your cat doesn't like drinking from a dish, give him a glass filled to the brim, and I bet he will drink much more.

## Cats are notoriously fussy eaters. Why is that, and should you humor them? If all you have is $1.99 generic cat food, won't they eat it eventually to avoid starving?

The old adage that "hunger is the best sauce" is demonstrated to anyone who has watched a starving street cat jump into a Dumpster to eat

garbage. A well-fed, pampered house cat may turn up his nose at cat food because he knows you are going to give him deli ham instead. However, no healthy animal will voluntarily starve itself to death. If you insist that your cat eat cat food instead of deli ham, he will—maybe not with the same gusto of a starving cat, but eventually he will give in and eat it.

## What is the best material for a cat's food bowl? Are plastic bowls harmful?

You wouldn't think that plastic cat bowls would be harmful, but some plastics can leak formaldehyde, which can discolor a cat's nose. Many times, the grease from cat food gets into microscopic scratches in plastic bowls. This causes bacteria to grow, and when the cat's chin touches the bowl, the cat can develop an infection. That will look like acne along his jaw. This can be eliminated by using a ceramic or stainless steel bowl and washing it thoroughly every time you use it. In nature, cats eat prey without their mouths even touching the ground.

## Would my cat like some fresh fish? Should it be fed cooked or raw?

The domestic cat's ancestor, the North African wild cat, would have never had access to fish in the deserts of Egypt and Libya. This is not a natural food for any cat aside from the Asian fishing cat, which is a wild animal. But fish is protein, which is good for cats. Use your own judgment and consult your vet about whether to feed it raw or cooked.

## Is it true that a cat might ignore his food bowl if it's not wide enough?

It depends on how hungry the cat is. Cats don't like any discomfort. If his bowl is so small that his whiskers hang over the edge, he will be uncomfortable eating from it. Personally, I have found that cats prefer wider bowls that can accommodate their whiskers.

## Living with a Crazy Cat

Almost every cat can be trained to reliably use a litter box, but every once in a while you do come across a cat that is truly hopeless. About ten years ago, I became the recipient of an enormous black half-Persian crazy cat that was originally found as a stray in Moscow, adopted, and imported into New York when her rescuers emigrated from Russia— and eventually foisted on me through no fault of my own. Her name was Nastia, and the owner told me this was short for Anastasia. But after I had her for a couple of weeks, I believed it was just Russian for *nasty*. She is the nastiest cat I have ever met. If you are walking past her, she will rake your leg with her claws just for the fun of it. She has no tolerance for any other animal and refuses to use a litter box. What a delightful pet! She is, however, one of the prettiest cats I've ever seen.

For years, we tried to incorporate her into our normal home routine. This wreaked havoc with our other animals and us. She loved to jump onto the dining room table, and since she weighed 25 pounds, she would just spread out and take up half the table. If my wife tried to get her off to serve dinner, Nastia would lash out and scratch her. Spraying her with a water bottle had no effect on her. Instead of getting off the table, she would just roll onto her back so you could spray her belly. I think she must be part otter, or maybe Russian cats like water. Next, I tried putting a scat mat on the table; this is a small plastic mat with electrodes and a nine-volt battery. It produces a mild shock if a cat or dog touches it, and it is usually a very effective deterrent to keep an animal off the furniture (however, it's a last resort for behavior problems—but better to try this than to relinquish the animal). I put the mat on the dining room table, but Nastia would just lie on top of it. At first I thought it wasn't working, but when I touched it, I got shocked. Maybe living on the streets of Moscow made her impervious to pain.

While none of these behaviors is pleasant, we were willing to tolerate them, but her refusal to use a litter box was another matter. We tried for years to train her. Sometimes she will poop in the litter box, and sometimes she pees on a wee-wee pad, but she definitely has issues. After ten years of trying, these issues have not changed.

Consequently, we can't leave Nastia loose in our home. We had no choice but to confine her to a large cage. It is 5 feet by 3 feet by 2 1/2 feet. Crate training a cat doesn't work quite the same as crate training a dog, but cats can definitely learn to live happily inside a cage. Since we could not train her to use the litter box, we crate trained her instead. In many situations, this is the best alternative, especially if the cat faces being taken to an animal shelter. In her cat cage, Nastia has a bed, shelves, perches, a scratching post, and a litter box where she will poop. Even in the cage, she absolutely refuses to pee in the litter box, so we have to put a wee-wee pad on the floor.

For half an hour each day, my wife lets Nastia out, and she will lie in the sun or on the table, but then it's back in the cage. Brushing her is impossible. And since she does have that thick coat, every couple of months I will wrap her in a blanket and hold her down while my wife goes through her coat and cuts out the mats in her fur.

I have no idea how old she is, but her teeth are pearly white and she has never had any medical problems, so it looks like she will be around for quite a while.

So don't complain if your cat has a little accident and tinkles on a pillow every now and then. After living with Nastia for all these years, you will get very little sympathy from me. She can top any complaint you might have about your cat's potty behavior.

## Will my cats be able to share the same litter box?

This depends on how many cats you have. In our house, we have six litter boxes. I think you should always have at least one extra. What if one cat wants to use it and another one is in there? Rather than waiting his turn, he may decide to poop on your bed instead. Also, some cats don't like to use a litter box that another cat recently used.

## Can cats really be trained to use the toilet? I sure never met one that did this!

Actually, they can. But doing this requires having a litter box right next to the toilet and a toilet seat on the edge of the litter box. Little by little, raise the toilet seat off the litter box so the cat loses the desire to bury his waste. This is a very unnatural way for a cat to eliminate, and I would imagine most cats would cheerfully choose another spot if they have the opportunity, such as throw rug, bed, or cushion. And I cannot imagine anyone having the time to teach the cat to do this. But if you have the time and the cat cooperates—good for you!

## Can cats get sick by licking clumping clay litter off their paws?

I'm sure that ingesting sufficient quantities of any clay litter would cause problems for a cat. However, if the litter was toxic, it would not be sold. Licking a little kitty litter here and there is not going to cause a problem, but it is not meant to be eaten in large quantities, no matter what kind you use.

Some cats do develop fetishes about eating certain substances. If your cat's litter is sticking to his paws to the extent that he is eating a noticeable amount of it to get it off, switch to another litter! There are only 40 billion of them on the market.

## Can I train an outdoor cat to use a litter box indoors?

Of course you can. The easiest way to train an outdoor cat to use a litter box is to first use a litter box of dirt from the backyard. This gives the cat something familiar. When he is reliably eliminating in the litter box full of dirt, little by little replace the dirt with kitty litter. Every cat is different. Some cats may need an entire box of dirt, others may accept a litter box of half dirt and half litter, some may accept a box of litter with just a handful of dirt, and some will immediately use the litter box with no training.

However, an outdoor cat will do his best to get back outside whenever the opportunity arises. You will need to do some fancy footwork when entering and leaving the house. As time goes on, if the cat never gets an opportunity to go back outside, he will forget this was ever an option.

The amount of time needed to train an outdoor cat to stay indoors will vary. Some outdoor cats do their best to get into the house and never want to go out again because there are dangers outside. Some cats go crazy when they are denied access to the outdoors. The key is to prevent the cat from getting outside. If he tries twenty times to get out of the house and manages to escape on the twenty-first try, he will conclude that he always needs to try this twenty-one times. The more consistent you are in the training, the quicker your cat will resign himself to the situation.

## Sometimes there's a present for me right outside the litter box. Did my cat just "miss" or is something wrong?

Maybe the litter box is too small for the cat or it was too dirty. For some reason, the cat decided not to use it, but he still had to go, so he went on the floor. It's your job as a pet keeper to determine what the problem was. Some cats prefer two litter boxes next to each other, one to urinate in and one to poop in. They won't use the same box for both. You have to give this type of cat more options so he doesn't choose the option of pooping on the floor.

### I've heard a general rule is to have a box for each cat plus one. If I have two cats in a small apartment, can I get around this?

Just because it's a general rule doesn't mean it will work in your house. If you have only one litter box but you completely change it every day so it stays nice and clean, that might work out well. If not, you will notice because there will be cat pee on your furniture.

There is always a place to hide one more litter box if you need it. Some litter boxes are designed to look like furniture. Once, when I was at Martha Stewart's house, I was in the bathroom and suddenly a cat came out from under the sink. Martha had made a little curtain around the sink and put a litter box under there. If she can have a litter box under the sink with a curtain around it, I'm sure you could, too.

### I heard that you can catch toxoplasmosis from cleaning the kitty litter box. Is this true? Is it dangerous?

This is a hot topic, and I have studied it exhaustively. You cannot catch toxoplasmosis from your indoor-only house cat that is using an indoor litter box. First of all, even if the cat did happen to have toxoplasmosis and he pooped in the litter box, it would take several days for the feces to become infectious. You are more likely to contract toxoplasmosis through accidental contact with cat

feces that stray cats might leave in your flower beds. These cats are more likely to be potential carriers, and the feces were probably there for a longer time, at which point they would be infectious.

This is a zoonotic disease caused by the microorganism *Toxoplasma gondii*. Cats can contract toxoplasmosis from eating infected prey or raw meat; pork is currently considered the primary source of infection in the United States. Cats are the only definitive host, and as a result the cat is the only species capable of shedding the infective oocytes of these protozoa. Most infected cats are asymptomatic. A few experience mild diarrhea or loss of appetite. Similarly, healthy humans who contract the infection develop only mild flulike symptoms. However, an infection can cause serious consequences for pregnant women and their unborn children.

Essentially, if your cat lives indoors, you clean the litter box daily, and you wear gloves when doing it, you have no reason to worry about toxoplasmosis. Even so, people still tend to worry. When my wife was pregnant, we had eight cats at home, and some of my family members became extremely neurotic about this. The only way to keep peace in the family was to assure everyone that my wife would not be cleaning any of the litter boxes; I would attend to them myself. In situations like this, some people are simply beyond reason, and it's just easier to agree. You can't fight City Hall.

## I had my cat neutered, but he is still spraying all over the house. Will this ever stop?

This depends on the cat. If he was neutered at a young age, the spraying should stop. If he was older when he was altered, he has a lot of testosterone circulating through his body. Or, if the spraying is motivated by

### SELF-CLEANING BOXES
Obviously, some cats are using them or they wouldn't be for sale, but some cats might be afraid of them. If you are concerned about this, start by putting out the self-cleaning box without plugging it in so the cat can get accustomed to it. Once the cat is comfortable, plug it in and run the self-cleaning mechanism.

a behavioral rather than a sexual issue, it will be hard to stop. Sometimes cats spray because of anxiety caused by a change in the household, such as a new person or pet brought into the home. Sometimes a stray cat outside the house can cause a cat to become territorial and urine-mark inside.

First, take your cat to the vet to rule out a medical issue. If he's healthy, try keeping him confined to one small room or a large cage, which will force the cat to use a litter box consistently. If you do this for many months, the cat will eventually forget about spraying objects in the house. Hope that when you then turn him loose in the house, he won't resume the habit.

## Is it possible to live with an intact male indoors? How do you deal with the spraying and marking? Why does it smell so bad and linger for so long when males spray?

When I was a kid, no one had neutered cats. We had plenty of tom cats around, and spraying in the house was never much of an issue. They used the litter box in the house but also had outdoor access every day. They were only indoors at night or during bad weather, so they had plenty of opportunities to spray their territory. Indoors, they seemed to understand there was no reason to do this, and they willingly used a litter box. As a very small child, I recall wondering why my male cat would squat in the litter box indoors but would stand up outside—spraying urine behind him! My parents could never quite explain this to me. At the time, there were no resources to explain that when this cat was outside, he was spraying his urine to notify the other male cats of his territory.

The urine of most carnivorous animals is extremely strong smelling because of the high protein concentration. It's meant to have a long-lasting strong smell. A cow urinates strictly to eliminate; it has no other meaning. But the cat wants all of the other cats to know who he is and where he is, and he uses his urine to announce these things to his rivals and potential mates.

However, today, keeping an intact tom cat indoors 24/7 is just not going to work. Most cat breeders that I know keep their tom cats in large cages or a

### EXTRA! EXTRA!

I personally buy cat litter made from recycled newsprint such as Yesterday's News. I find it to be less dusty and more absorbent. But use whatever works best for your cat and your lifestyle. I look for a brand that doesn't produce a lot of dust. I also like heavier litters because they don't stick to the cat's paws as he leaves the litter box.

## How do cats communicate with their tails?

In general, a cat walking around with his tail straight up is in a good mood. A cat with his tail down is being assertive, and a cat whose tail is whipping from side to side or "bottle brush" is definitely agitated. Only domestic cats will carry their tails up. All wild cats hold their tails down. I've seen many photos taken

in England and America of large black cats that were mistaken for escaped panthers. However, the cats in all of these pictures were holding their tails up, and no black panther would carry its tail this way.

## My cat likes to jump in the shower with me—what's up with that?

Some cats like water, including yours. Film it and share the video online.

## I just moved, and my cat is freaking out—hiding during the day, wandering around and howling at night, not eating, and not using the litter box as much. How long will this last, and what can I do to help her? (My other cat doesn't seem to care one whit, by the way.)

It will last until the cat feels that she is in a familiar place. Keep the cat in a "safe room," surrounded by her familiar things, including her litter box, so she can get used to one space at a time. Beyond that, you can't do much else other than ensure that food and water are available. She won't starve herself;

she is eating just enough to keep herself going. Once she realizes that this is home, she will settle down. Trying to comfort the cat won't help her make this determination, but that doesn't mean you should give up. Supplying the cat's favorite blanket, bed, or toys (and their familiar scents) from your previous home may help ease the transition. Of course, every cat is different, and if your cat does seem dehydrated or overly thin, you should take her to the vet just to make sure that her health isn't compromised during this adjustment period.

## Why do cats knead their paws?

When kittens nurse, they knead their mother's abdomen on each side of the nipples to stimulate milk flow. Since most cats think of us as their mothers, they often revert to kittenlike behavior when they spend time with us.

Some cats get carried away and will actually grab a piece of your clothing and suck on it. Although this behavior may seem nice, it can become a fetish. Most house cats have too much time on their hands, and obsessive behavior should be discouraged. If you cat starts this, it's better to put him on the floor and distract him with a toy or activity.

## Why do lots of cats seem to like crinkly noises?

It's not so much the crinkly noise. These sounds usually mean crinkly paper, and many cats have a paper fetish. They love playing in paper bags because they love the texture. Many cats also love bubble wrap. When they hear a crinkly noise, they associate it with these things they love, just as they associate the sound of a can opener with dinnertime.

## Why do cats do the "elevator butt" when you scratch their backs?

The cat's back is extremely sensitive. When you pet him, especially when you apply pressure to the base of the tail, the cat rears up to meet your hand to increase that pressure. Some cats become overly sensitive and forget what's going on. They will lash out and scratch or bite you because they get so stimulated. Every cat is an individual, but if your cat is really turned on by this sort of touching, it's a good idea to stop before the cat loses control.

## Why must my cat lie on only the papers I happen to be reading?

Cats are addicted to texture, and the smell and texture of a new newspaper appeals to many cats. When you spread out the paper to read it, your cat thinks you did this for his enjoyment. He has no idea that the paper has any value to you. To him, it's just something to play with.

Look at it from the cat's point of view. The first time this happened, you probably thought it was cute, so now the cat thinks it's OK to do it all the time. If you read your newspaper at the table and don't want the cat on the table, never let him up there. Every time he jumps up, put him on the floor. Eventually, after you do this 222 times, the cat will realize that there is no point to this.

## If my cat has such hardwired hunting instincts, why does she never "finish off" what she catches? Most of the time, she just looks as if she doesn't know what to do with herself.

It's natural for cats to kill small birds and rodents. Some eat the whole animal, some eat only the heads, and some bring their prey back to their owners as a present. Instinct

motivates her to kill. She isn't eating her prey because she is not hungry enough. I remember the first time I saw one of my cats kill a bird and eat it when I was a kid. He crunched it down and swallowed the whole thing, feathers and all. This cat always ate everything he caught. The only food he got from me was dry cat food; his hunting satisfied his meat cravings.

I bought my new cat some fun, colorful toys at the pet store, but all he wants to play with are some used cotton swabs, broken shoelaces, and bottle caps he's pulled from the trash. Is this normal?

You answered this question yourself. From an animal's point of view, what's the difference between things from the trash and things you brought home from the store and threw on the floor? Obviously, the items from the trash have a better smell or texture, and they appeal to the cat more than the items from the pet store. If the trash is more fun to play with, compare it with the store-bought toys and try to figure out why. Then you can choose toys that fit the bill. Or you can keep the trash locked up so the cat can't play with it. Then he will be forced to play with what you give him.

## My cat has laid claim to the hall closet, and he attacks us when we try to get him out. Do we need to build another closet?

There is something about the closet that appeals to the cat, so the best approach is to make the closet unappealing to the cat. First, take out everything piled on the floor and shelves of that closet. Purchase some plastic carpet runners at a home-supply store, and cut sections to fit the size of the floor and shelves. Lay them upside down so that the bumps are facing up. Now, instead of having boxes and shoes and hats to hide behind like before, the cat will have only barren surfaces covered in hard, bumpy plastic. The cat will then decide that the hall closet was a great place to live, but not anymore. Once he's over it, resume use of the closet.

The easiest way to revise a cat's behavior is to trick him into thinking your idea is his idea. In pet politics, sometimes you need to be a little sneaky.

## Why does my cat always try to eat her blanket? I've tried taking it away from her, but she goes crazy looking for it.

Some cats, particularly Siamese cats, have fetishes for different fabrics—especially wool. I once had a Siamese cat named Trouble that had a very strong wool fetish. When we had guests over, I would have to hide their wool coats in the closet. If I laid them on the bed, Trouble would eat half of their coats by the end of the night.

No one knows why a fetish starts or how to stop it. All you can do is prevent it. If your cat is eating his blanket rather than your clothes (or anything else valuable), and this behavior is not causing any physical problems for the cat, I would just let him have the blanket. If you would rather he didn't eat the blanket, I would just get rid of it and let him go nuts for three or four days. Then he will forget that the blanket ever existed. It's your choice.

## How can I stop my cat from begging during dinner? She jumps right onto the table and tries to take food from our plates.

She does it because she can. If the cat jumps onto the table nine times and you remove her from the table nine times, but on the tenth time you give in and give her a bit of food, she will realize that she will succeed every ten tries. If you kept a spray bottle on the dinner table and sprayed her every time she jumped up, she would soon realize that her approach isn't yielding the desired results. Animals only do what works for them. If jumping onto the table works, she will do it. If it doesn't work, why should she expend the energy?

With eight cats loose in my house, we always have a spray bottle handy. The only exception I ever made was for my elderly Siamese cat Rocky. He was a tabby point Siamese, a very frail kitten that I nursed back to health. I loved him dearly. When Rocky was alive, many times I would come home from work really late at night. My wife would reheat my dinner, and I would sit and eat in the kitchen, all alone. Rocky would come out of nowhere and jump on the table and just sit next to me. He wouldn't beg, or meow, or try to take my food. He just enjoyed my company and sat there until I was done. I would save him the last morsel on my plate, and he would delicately take it like the gentleman that he was. I cried for weeks after he died.

---

### BODY LANGUAGE

With the exception of tail gestures, canine and feline body languages are pretty similar. When a dog wags his tail, we know he is friendly. When a cat does this, it indicates anger. Apart from that, there are not too many differences. An arched back with raised hackles indicates fear in both cats and dogs; ears flattened back indicates aggression or fear.

---

## My cat was attacked by a stray cat in my yard. Now she is afraid to go outside. What can I do?

Anyone who has been attacked is going to feel upset. Perhaps you don't see the stray cat in your yard any longer, but he may still be there. He may leave scent markings, or your cat may hear him. Whatever the reason, your cat is not convinced that it's safe out there. Actually, most cats are not safe outdoors anyway. So if your cat wants to stay in the house,

encourage her to do so. Cats will not go anywhere they don't feel safe, and only the cat can decide if a particular area is safe.

## My cat hates going in the car, and whenever I bring out the carrier, she knows what's up and hides. How can I get her to accept this occasional part of life?

Many owners avoid taking their cats to the vet because the trip is such a horrible ordeal for both the cats and the owners. It's silly to compromise your cat's veterinary care for this reason. When you think about it, cats have traveled with humans all over the world via every kind of transportation. A cat can adapt to travel just like anything else in its life. Cats instinctively fear the unknown because they live longer that way. Once the unknown becomes known, the fear disappears.

Pet cats develop a negative association with their carriers because they rarely get to travel, and the few times that they do, they are taken someplace unpleasant. I've driven all over the eastern United States with my cats in carriers, and they are very comfortable in them.

Instead of taking the carrier out only when the cat is going to the vet, let the cat get used to the carrier in a positive way. Put it in the living room, leave the door open, and give the cat a chance to become familiar with it. Put the cat's bed in there and let her go in and out, and eventually she will realize that it's not a bad thing. This is the same way you would train a dog to accept a crate. Instead of putting a blanket inside, cover the bottom with a thick layer of shredded newspaper. This way, the cat can nestle in the paper. If the cat has only a blanket, the blanket will slide to the corner when the carrier tilts, and the cat will have nothing to sit on.

Periodically, put the cat in the carrier and go somewhere that has no

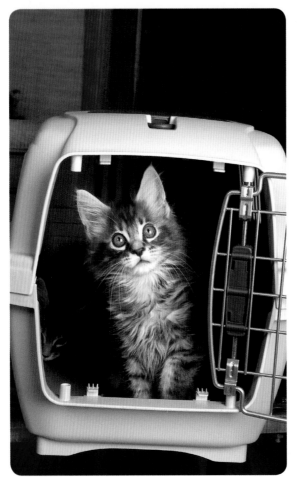

negative connotations for her. Take her to the pet shop for some toys and treats. If you take the cat many different places in the carrier, she won't associate it with something bad, and she won't fear the unknown—because it will no longer be unknown. If, every now and then, the cat must go to the vet in the carrier, that's just a random event in life that the cat will learn to accept.

On my weekly Sirius satellite radio show, *Ask Marc, the Pet Keeper*, I get many calls from truck drivers who travel with cats in the cabs of their trucks. These cats lead fine lives; they have litter boxes and beds, and they travel all over the country this way. It's a kitty convoy, so to speak.

## Why does my cat sleep so much?

Anyone who has seen the lions on Animal Planet shows knows that they sleep most of the time when they are not eating, hunting, or mating. Cats are basically small lions, so they operate on the same schedule. For most predatory animals, procuring food uses up a tremendous amount of energy, so they must sleep for long periods to recoup that energy. House cats really don't need to follow this protocol, but it is instinctive. Until they can learn how to surf the Internet, cats will probably continue conforming to this instinctive pattern and sleep all day. In my house, cats seem to be sleeping every time I look at them.

## Will my cat get separation anxiety if I leave him home alone all day?

True separation anxiety is actually pretty rare in animals. If an animal destroys the house because he's bored and unsupervised, it's easy to label this as separation anxiety. That lets the pet keeper off the hook for not socializing, training, and supervising the pet. If your cat is destroying things when you are not home, this is more likely because he is bored and you were negligent in leaving these valuable items within his reach.

There are some behavioral disorders attributable to a true chemical imbalance in the brain. It does happen, but it's the vet's job to determine this. He can then prescribe the appropriate medication if it is called for. When it comes to animal behavior, the simplest, most straightforward answer is usually the right one. Our lives are so complicated, and we sometimes think this is also true of our animals. Their needs, however, are very cut-and-dried.

## COUCH POTATO KITTY?

I have personally never had a cat that watched TV, but I have stacks of photographs I've received from people showing their cats glued to the tube. Veterinary ophthalmologists have explained to me that cats have rods and cones in their eyes.

The number of rods and cones determines what they can see. Vision varies from person to person, so I expect this is also true of cats. So some cats watch TV, and others don't. No one really knows why.

## Why does my cat play-bite so much, and how can I encourage him to quit it?

The cat play-bites because you let him. If the kitten did this to his mother, she would swat him on the head and that would be the end of it. You probably let your cat do this when he was little. As he got bigger, he was able to bite harder. If you are petting your cat and he starts getting too excited, stop before he bites you. Put him on the floor and redirect him to a toy. The best toy for a cat to bite can't be found in the pet shop; every sock drawer holds some lonely single socks that make wonderful cat toys.

Fill a long sock with balls of crumpled newspaper. Fill the whole thing and pour a bottle of catnip in there. Tie the sock shut, attach a piece of string, and pull it along the floor. The cat will have a great time pouncing on the sock. He will go nuts when he hears the paper crinkle; this sound triggers something in the cat's psyche. A toy like this will redirect the cat's play behavior to an inanimate object.

## I know cats aren't supposed to like water, but can they swim if they have to?

Almost any quadruped animal can swim; even sloths can swim. Any cat that finds himself in the water will instinctively use his tail as a rudder and paddle. Cats may not like water the way an otter, muskrat, or beaver does, but a cat

can certainly swim to shore provided the currents aren't too strong. In fact, many movie cats are trained to swim simply by habituating them to the water.

Some cat breeds, such as the Turkish Van, instinctively like water. And many individual cats like water very much.

## Your Cat's Veterinarian

When I was a kid, the idea of taking a cat to a veterinarian was unheard of. If a cat got sick, everyone agreed that it was a pity, and the cat crawled off into the woods and died. The idea of neutering a male cat, or dog for that matter, was considered totally absurd. Female cats were only spayed when our mothers became 150 percent fed up with kittens all over the place twice a year. Only if a female cat was exceptionally beloved would household money be allotted to have her spayed.

One of my friends constantly had thirty or more cats, although they were never allowed in the house. However, he had two acres of property, so there was plenty of room for the cats. But you couldn't drive past his house without noticing cats draped all over the place. They were well cared for, but this never included veterinary care. New kittens were regularly born, and older cats were killed by raccoons and foxes or hit by cars.

It's not that there weren't any veterinarians around to take care of cats in those days. In urban areas, cats were taken to the vet if they got sick, but never to the extent that this is done today. Back then, you only took a cat to the vet as a last resort, and often by then there was little that could be done for him.

The technology of feline veterinary medicine has advanced a thousandfold in the last forty years, and we are new accustomed to proactive rather than reactive veterinary care for our cats. Most cat owners take their pets to the vet for regular checkups in order to catch health problems in their early stages. Cats are extremely adept at hiding their symptoms, which is why it is so important to take your cat to the vet each year to have his teeth cleaned, have blood drawn, and simply allow your vet to compare the results of each year's physical exam. This gives the vet a chance to discover anything before it blossoms into a full-blown health problem.

Keep in mind that vets are like any other group of people; some are good and some not so good. Some good vets don't communicate very well with people; some bad vets do. Since your cat can't talk to the vet, you must be his voice. Your cat cannot pick up the phone and call the vet. Most cats don't even like to show that they are sick. So it is your responsibility as a cat keeper to utilize the technology that is available to help your cat live a long and healthy life.

If you have questions or you don't understand something that the vet says, don't walk out of his office until you have the information you need. Many people send me questions or call my radio show with questions about their cats that should have been answered by their vet. When I question them, I find out that they were too embarrassed or intimidated to ask the vet to explain something they needed to know. Either they didn't understand the explanation the vet gave them, or they felt hesitant about taking up more of the vet's time.

People tend to consider me quite erudite about pet keeping, but if I don't understand something about my pet's health, I don't hesitate to ask more questions. I have no problem admitting to my vet that I didn't understand something he told me. I ask him to explain it in a way that a simpleton like me can understand. If I'm not too embarrassed to say this, you shouldn't be, either. If the vet is too busy, I tell him that I have more questions, and I ask for a good time to call him and discuss it further.

These days, we also have pet health insurance. Veterinary care is very expensive, so it's nice to know that in the event of an emergency, your insurance will compensate you for some of the costs. I highly recommend it for all pet keepers.

My cat has always been nervous and high-strung. I've noticed that if I leave the house for long periods of time, I return to a pile of vomit. Is it possible she thinks I've left for good and that's what's upsetting her? What can I do to calm her? Should I put her on kitty tranquilizers?

When a cat is upset and panicky, whatever comes out of the cat will come out of the other end. If your cat is vomiting, that is a medical or dietary issue. It has nothing to do with the cat's mental state. Some cats that eat only dry food will swallow it without chewing it well. If it becomes mixed with fur in the cat's stomach, it will come up as a mixture of fur and undigested cat food. But this has nothing to do with stress. You should see your veterinarian about this.

## How can I tell if my cat is too fat?

In general, if the cat looks fat, he is. If your first impression is *fat* rather than *cat*, he is probably fat. With dogs, the rule is that you should be able to feel the ribs under the coat, but this doesn't really work with cats. Each cat is a little different, and his muscle structure is different. If you are not sure, ask your vet.

## How do I know if my cat has hairballs?

You will know because you will probably find them in your shoe in the morning. As a general rule, cats that eat dry food tend to regurgitate hairballs more frequently than cats that are fed canned or raw-food diets do. Many cats don't chew dry food properly, and this partially chewed food ends up mixing with fur in the cat's stomach. This forms a mass that is vomited up a few hours later. We consider this a hairball, but in reality it is the undigested food taking the hair out of the cat's digestive tract.

Unless you x-ray the cat's stomach, there is no way to tell if he has hairballs. Sooner or later, they will come out of one end of the cat or the other. Then you will know that your cat *had* hairballs.

## Do hairball-formula cat foods really work? What is the best way to get rid of hairballs?

These cat food formulas contain soy lecithin, which really does help break up the fats and proteins in the cat's stomach and prevent the fur from clumping into hairballs. This makes it easier for everything to pass through the cat's intestines and end up in the litter box, rather than being vomited into your shoe in the middle of the night. However, the best way to prevent hairballs is to groom your cat frequently and remove loose fur before the cat can ingest it.

There are many petroleum-based supplements sold in pet stores that will coat the hair, making it easier for it to pass through the cat's digestive tract. These are usually flavored with malt, and cats seem to like them. If you try one of these supplements and your cat doesn't like it, smear a little on his paw so that he is forced to lick it off. Don't use a big blob, as he will just shake his foot, and the blob will end up on the wall. Massage it into his fur so he must lick it off.

This was actually an old-time trick used to acclimate a cat to a new home. When you brought a new cat home and didn't want him to wander away from your property, you would rub butter all through his fur and put him on your porch. He would be forced to spend hours licking all of the butter out of his coat before he could run away and try to find his old home. By the time he finished getting the butter out of his fur, he would decide that his new home was an OK place to stay after all.

## My cat's tongue feels like sandpaper. Why do cats have such rough tongues?

A cat's tongue is rough because it needs to be that way. Some wild cats have such rough tongues that they can literally lick your skin off. When a cat eats raw meat, the little barbs on his tongue help pull the bits of meat off the bones. The barbs also help the cat pull loose fur out of his coat. When God created cats, I'm sure He didn't realize that they would be

living in our homes and licking us with their barbed tongues. If He had known, He probably would have made their tongues a little smoother.

## Do cats pant to keep cool the way dogs do?

They certainly do, but we rarely see them doing this. Cats are smart enough to stay out of the heat. When it's really hot out, you will never see a cat running around in the sun the way dogs often do. The cat will be sleeping behind the toilet bowl on the cool tile floor or hidden under a bush in the shade. Dogs have such a strong desire to please us, they will compromise their welfare, and this is why we see them walking around panting in the summer. Cats disappear when it gets hot out. But they do pant and sweat through their paws, both of which dogs do.

## My dog is on heartworm medication. Should I get this for my cat, too?

Heartworm is not as common in cats as it is in dogs, and they typically harbor fewer heartworms than dogs do. But cats can get heartworm in exactly the same way that it is transmitted to dogs: by mosquitoes. It is also prevented in the same way. If you live in an area where heartworm is prevalent, ask your veterinarian if you should put your cat on heartworm preventative. Heartworm is not contagious, but it is seen more frequently now, since many infected Hurricane Katrina cats were relocated to areas where heartworm was previously uncommon.

## What is the easiest way to give a cat a pill?

It's really, really hard to give a cat a pill. The pill must be very small. I dip it in heavy cream first. Open the cat's mouth by putting your fingers behind the incisor teeth, then push the pill over the cat's tongue and hold his mouth closed. You won't know the pill has gone down until you see the tip of his tongue sticking out. I've had my finger bitten many times doing this. It is much easier to get a pill gun from your vet. This is a plastic device that holds the pill. It has a plunger that you can depress to get the pill down the cat's throat.

You may still need help. As a general rule, giving a cat a pill is a two-person job—one person to hold the cat and one to poke the pill down. Have someone wrap the cat tightly in a blanket so he is swathed in a cocoon. Dip the pill in cream, put it in the pill gun, open the cat's mouth, pop the pill gun over the cat's tongue, depress the plunger, and keep the cat's mouth closed until you see the tip of his tongue protrude. For some cats, it takes three people, one to hold the cat, one to open his mouth, and one to give the pill.

Some medications may be compromised by dairy products, so check with your vet before using cream as a lubricant. In that case, you can try using flavored gelatin pill pockets to hide the pill. Some cats willingly take these, but not all do.

If possible, ask your vet if there is a liquid medication you can give instead of pills. For most cats, this is much easier.

## My cat won't stop sneezing. Is she allergic to something?

Respiratory problems in cats are as varied as cats themselves. Only your veterinarian can determine what the problem may be. Many cats harbor low-grade respiratory infections that cause sneezing. Certain parasites such as lungworm can also cause respiratory symptoms. You really need to get an accurate diagnosis from a vet.

## I have one indoor cat that has never been interested in going outside. Does he still need shots every year?

Only your vet can tell you that. Most likely, the vet will first do a blood test, called a titer test, to determine precisely what antibodies are in the cat's system. If the antibody titer test shows that the cat is adequately protected, then the cat does not need additional vaccinations. However, every pet should be seen by a vet each year for an annual wellness check regardless of whether he needs to be vaccinated.

## I heard that rabies shots cause cancer in cats. Is this true?

All fifty states require dogs to be vaccinated against rabies, but not many states require rabies vaccinations for cats. Vaccine-site carcinoma was first described about thirty years ago. I think that Pennsylvania had mandated that all cats be vaccinated against rabies. This led to a sudden increase in the number of cats developing an inflammatory response and sarcoma after the vaccination. The University of Pennsylvania first reported this and made definite connections between the vaccination and the incidence of cancer. This is definitely true.

However, if your cat goes outdoors and regularly encounters wildlife, you probably should have your cat vaccinated. Raccoons, foxes, and other predators can carry and transmit rabies. This is very common in North America. You can also run into legal problems if your cat bites or scratches someone and he has not been vaccinated against rabies.

Rabies vaccines may be administered annually or every three years. However, a smart pet keeper will first have the vet run a rabies titer test to determine if the cat needs a booster shot. I export cats to other countries for owners who are moving. Rather than requiring that the cat get an unnecessary vaccination, many countries will accept a blood titer test showing that the cat has adequate protection against rabies.

Rabies vaccination remains a debatable topic, and many people tend to be adamant about their views. You should do your own research and discuss it with your vet. Certain vaccinations are essential, but this should never be a casual decision.

## I don't want to give my cat too many vaccinations. Which ones does he really need?

Kittens should receive their first vaccinations when they are six weeks old; these should be followed up by additional vaccinations every three to four weeks until they are sixteen weeks of age. There are core vaccines and noncore vaccines. Core vaccines protect against diseases that most cats are exposed to, such as feline panleukemia, feline herpes virus, feline calicivirus, and rabies. These vaccines will protect the kitten from a range of viruses. For adult cats, the rabies vaccine is probably the most important, especially if our cat goes outdoors and risks potential exposure to rabid wildlife.

### TAURINE

Taurine is an essential nutrient for most mammals that is synthesized from two amino acids. It plays an important role in digestion of fats and retinal function for normal eyesight. Taurine is only found in animal protein. Meat, poultry, and fish all contain high concentrations of it. Unlike dogs, cats can synthesize only small amounts of taurine, so they need a consistent dietary supply of it. Monkeys, rabbits, and guinea pigs also have limited ability to synthesize taurine, but only cats can suffer a serious deficiency because they require so much of it. If cats don't get enough, they can develop retinal degeneration, leading to blindness. This is why cats are considered obligate carnivores, meaning that they must eat other animals in order to survive. Many vegans have tried to create vegan diets for cats with only moderate success. Realistically, if you are a vegan and you feel that your beliefs are compromised by keeping meat in your home to feed your cat, you should consider keeping a vegetarian animal as a pet.

Noncore feline vaccines include those for feline immunodeficiency virus, feline infectious peritonitis, feline chlamydiosis, and feline leukemia virus. Some vets consider these important and others don't, depending on what they regularly encounter in their practices.

## Is it true that cats can get AIDS and leukemia? Should I get my cat vaccinated to protect him?

While cats are susceptible to feline leukemia and feline AIDS (FIV), these diseases have no relation to the human forms. And although there are vaccines to protect against them, these diseases are more prevalent in certain areas, and your veterinarian is in the best position to know whether they pose a threat to your cat. At one time, both of these diseases were very common, but in my area they don't seem to be much of an issue these days. Your vet is the one to advise you on what is best for your cat.

## I've heard that some foods and houseplants can be lethal to a cat? What would you say are the ones that most people don't realize?

Lilies are probably the most dangerous plants for cats, in addition to spider plants. Cats have been observed chewing on spider plants and subsequently drooling and vomiting. There is something in spider plants that causes these problems.

Lilies are toxic, causing irritation of the mouth and esophagus. In some cases, it can cause the cat's esophagus to swell and can even be fatal. Poinsettias, Christmas roses, and chrysanthemums can also have serious effects on cats. Foxglove is also dangerous. If the cat consumes foxglove, compounds from the plant will enter his bloodstream and affect his heart rate and respiration.

If you call the ASPCA Poison Control Hotline at 1-888-426-4435, you can get a complete list of potentially poisonous and toxic plants. Or consult their Web site: http://www.aspca.org/pet-care/poison-control/plants.

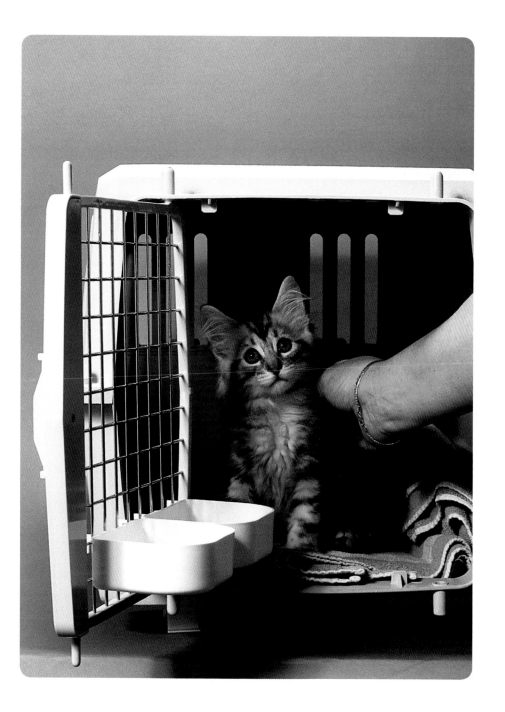

## Why is it that a cat's scratch can make you so sick?

Cats' nails are extremely sharp, and they harbor bacteria. When you get scratched, the nail acts almost as a hypodermic needle. The bacteria from the nail can be transferred deep into your skin and enter your bloodstream. This is sometimes called cat scratch fever, and it's something I have suffered from continually since age five. So I'm pretty sure it's not fatal—or perhaps I have just built up a resistance to the bacteria on cats' claws!

## What's a Jacobsen's organ?

Also known as the vomeronasal organ, this is an auxiliary olfactory sense organ located in the roof of the mouth, comprising a pair of small, fluid-filled sacs. It sits just behind the upper incisors and connects the mouth and the nasal passages. It contains chemical receptor cells, which can detect pheromones associated with sexual, social, and feeding behaviors.

When the cat smells specific odors, it triggers a behavior known as a Flehmen response. The cat will sniff and taste the odor by raising his head, drawing back his lips, and wrinkling his nose with his mouth partly open in order to inhale the scent directly to the Jacobsen's organ. This response isn't

often seen in domestic house cats today because they don't rely on this sense as much as their wild counterparts do. When I was a kid, there were many more unneutered cats, and I often saw tom cats do this when they caught a whiff of a female cat in heat. House cats that have been neutered or spayed are most likely to exhibit this response when they smell catnip.

## How many teeth does a cat have? Can cats smile the way dogs can?

Kittens have twenty-six baby teeth, and adult cats have thirty permanent teeth that emerge between four and

six months of age. You don't see your kitten's baby teeth when they fall out because they usually lose them when they are running around and playing. They fly out of the cat's mouth and end up under the radiator. They may also fall out while the kitten is eating, and he will just swallow it.

Cats may look as if they can smile, but this isn't technically a smile as we would think of it. When a cat is smiling, he lifts his upper lip to use his Jacobsen's organ to taste the air. If he happens to do this when he sees you, he is just trying to check out your smell.

## I've heard that cats often develop urinary-tract infections. What's the best way to make sure this doesn't happen to my cat?

Unfortunately, we can't prevent all bad things from happening to our cats. Years ago, most veterinarians assumed that the high ash content in commercial cat foods caused urinary stones and other problems in male cats. However, female cats are also subject to urinary-tract infections.

This is a major reason why cats have house-training accidents and refuse to use their litter boxes. A urinary-tract infection will cause the cat's private parts to be sensitive, and he will find it much more comfortable to urinate on a nice soft down comforter rather than inside a box of scratchy cat litter. Pelleted forms of litter such as recycled newspaper, wheat, or corn feel better than litter made from sharp, angular pieces.

The most important thing you can do to prevent this is to make sure that your cat drinks plenty of water. The worst way to encourage a cat to drink water is to use one of those double dishes with side-by-side compartments. The water will inevitably be contaminated with food particles and therefore be unappealing to the cat. Many cats also refuse to drink from small saucers because it is uncomfortable when their whiskers hit the edges of the dish. Conversely, some cats prefer drinking out of tall glasses because their whiskers never come in contact with anything. I have had cats that will only drink out of a glass filled to the brim and placed on a kitchen counter. Some cats will only drink running water, such as a leaky faucet. You can get little fountains

for cats that provide continuously circulating water. You need to be a little imaginative when trying to encourage your cat to drink enough water. Otherwise, the cat will be dehydrated, which will compromise his kidney function.

Urinary-tract problems are best prevented by feeding your cat the best possible diet and taking him for annual vet checks so that any problems can be detected before they become serious. A canned or raw diet is best for cats that are prone to these problems.

## Is it true that cats can get asthma? How is it treated?

One of my employees has a cat that suffers from feline asthma, and he has to take daily medication to control it. He can be fine for weeks, and then suddenly he has an attack and can't breathe at all. In these cases, his owner must immediately rush him to the vet for a shot. This cat, Louie, has had this condition for ten years and is doing just fine. The condition is manageable, but it does require veterinary care since the cat is not going to pull out an inhaler when he is having trouble breathing.

> ### FATTY LIVER DISEASE
> Technically known as hepatic lipidosis, this is the most common type of liver disease in cats. It causes an excessive accumulation of fat in the liver, which eventually causes liver failure. The cause is unknown, but it is more common in obese, diabetic cats. It can be triggered by a sudden dietary change, abrupt weight loss, or stressful event such as moving to a new home. Symptoms include vomiting, lethargy, loss of appetite, and jaundice. It is usually treated with supportive care to correct dehydration and encourage the cat to start eating again. It can be fatal, but with early treatment such a severe condition can usually be avoided.

## Moby Dick: the Killer Cat

The most difficult cat that I must regularly groom is an enormous polydactyl black male Maine Coon owned by one of my customers. This cat is 28 pounds of pure muscle. His poor owner has been banned from every veterinarian and pet groomer on Long Island because of Moby Dick's behavior. His owner calls him Moby Dick because he has a crooked jaw, just like Herman Melville's white whale. Even though his jaw is a little off-kilter, it is still full of big pearly white teeth, and he does not hesitate to use them.

Because he is polydactyl, he often needs his nails trimmed, but he is so big, so nasty, and so strong that I am the only person who can do this. Thus, we have devised a special method to clip Moby Dick's nails.

Moby Dick's owner brings him into my store in a special carrier on wheels because he is too heavy to be carried. She wheels him in, and I then must dismantle the carrier because there is no way I would attempt to get him out through the door. Once I have the top off the carrier, I throw a large blanket over him and literally straddle him. As he howls, hisses, spits, and carries on, I feel for each of his legs through the blanket. When I find one, I take a pair of scissors and cut a hole in the blanket to pull his paw through. I can then cut the nails on that foot. This means we must cut four holes in a blanket every time Moby Dick needs nail trimming, but his owner is content to keep buying cheap blankets at Kmart for this purpose.

In a perfect world, a cat like Moby Dick could be clicker-trained to desensitize him to having his nails trimmed. My friends who work in zoos do this with lions, tigers, cougars, and all sorts of exotic wild cats. They are trained to hold their paws through the bars to have their nails trimmed. I have even seen adult male lions back up to the bars of a cage to get a shot in exchange for the reward of a tasty piece of meat. Of course, the people who work in these zoos and institutions are paid to train animals all day. The lives of typical pet owners are so complicated and busy, we don't always have the time to spend on extensive training, so we need to seek shortcuts like throwing a blanket over Moby Dick and cutting four holes in it.

## Why does my cat start licking himself after missing a jump or falling off the windowsill? Is he just trying to save face?

Although we would like to think that cats are very proud animals, that is strictly a human emotion. Most likely when the cat falls off the windowsill, his fur is all messed up and covered with dust and he needs to rearrange his coat. The one human emotion I would like to attribute to cats is vanity. Cats hate to look bad. More likely, they just feel better when their fur is perfectly groomed. But allow me this one fantasy.

## I've had my indoor longhair cat for a few months, and all I've had to do is brush her once every day or two. Now, all of a sudden, she's getting a lot of mats. What's happening?

Well, she is indoors and she is a longhair cat. Long hair gets more matted indoors. The hair mats less outdoors because things like wind blowing through the coat keeps it from clumping together. Indoors, the long hair twists together and forms mats. This is very uncomfortable for the cat, so frequent combing with a stainless steel comb is important to separate the hair. Then you can fluff it out with a slicker brush.

The best grooming tool I have found for longhair cats is a stainless steel comb with rotating teeth, which spin as the comb is pulled through the cat's hair. But this is a hard item to find. Other stainless steel combs work as long as you comb the cat every day. Snow leopards and Siberian tigers have long hair, but it is stiff and straight. It doesn't form mats. Domestic longhair cats have loose, limp hair that will mat. This trait was developed by humans, so it's our responsibility to keep it in good condition.

Mats can be very hard to separate. I've found that rubbing them with Vaseline and separating them with your fingers can tease the mats apart if the cat will let you do this. If the cat is unwilling, then you need to go to a vet, have the cat anesthetized, have the mats cut out, and do anything else that the cat needs. From then on, you need to groom the cat every day to prevent the problem's recurrence.

## How many digits do cats normally have on their feet? Why are some cats polydactyls?

Cats and dogs normally have five digits on each front paw and four on each back paw. Some dogs have one digit on each front leg surgically removed after birth. This digit is called the dewclaw. Like some humans, animals can have extra digits due to a mutation. This is called polydactyly. In cats, this can cause problems because they don't have the ability to unsheathe the claws on these extra digits. Owners of polydactyl cats must trim these extra nails frequently to prevent them from growing around and puncturing the pad. The Ernest Hemingway estate in Key West, Florida, is full of polydactyl cats. I am sure the caretakers have a big job examining and trimming the nails of all of those cats.

## Whenever I try to brush my kitten, he tries to bite and bat at the brush. I wind up giving up after a while because he just won't sit still. What can I do?

He has learned that swatting the brush will make you leave him alone. You need to put the kitten in your lap and go over him with the brush, even if it is only for ten seconds. Don't let the kitten decide when the grooming session is over. You decide when to groom the cat and when the grooming session is over. As time goes on, increase the time you spend doing this until the cat accepts it.

If you go to a cat show, you will see all the longhair cats sitting patiently while their owners brush and groom them. These cats are used to it because their owners did it until the cats accepted it as a part of life. Domesticated animals can accept most anything as long as they understand that no harm will come to them—and that they have no choice in the matter.

## How often should I brush my cat's teeth?

The more often you brush them, the longer they will last. But if you have eight cats like I do, it is very hard to brush all of their teeth every day. I try to do one cat per day, so they are done on a weekly basis. In a perfect world, I would do this

every day, but they all have pretty good teeth. However, one of my older cats, Paulie, almost died because he had a rotted molar in back that I never noticed despite brushing his teeth for seventeen years. The molar rotted,

and the infection entered his bloodstream and almost killed him. The vet was able to extract the molar and put him on intravenous antibiotics, thus extending his life for a couple more years.

## I recently adopted an older cat from a shelter. Should I even attempt to brush her teeth, or should I assume that if she hasn't had this done since kittenhood, she won't tolerate it now?

The easiest way to brush a cat's teeth is to get some cat toothpaste and put a little bit on the cat's nose and mouth so he can get used to the taste. Do this for a few days until the cat realizes that this is something really good that he can cope with. Once the cat readily accepts having toothpaste on his nose, put some on your finger. Put your finger in the cat's mouth and let him lick it off. As he gets used to this step, start to massage his teeth and gums with your finger. In many cases, the friction from your finger, at least with my rough hands, is enough to get the cat's teeth clean. If not, wrap a little gauze around your finger and rub the cat's teeth with that. You can also get fingertip brushes that look like little thimbles. Put the toothpaste on one of these and gently massage the cat's teeth.

## Should I shave my longhair cat in the summer?

A longhair cat would feel more comfortable if he were shaved. However, this practice is not that common. Most people shave longhair cats more for their own benefit than for the cat's benefit. That way, they don't have to comb the cat or worry about his fur getting matted. Cats don't suffer the same discomfort from heat as dogs do, mainly because we don't force them to go outside when it's hot. Nor do they have the desire to accompany us anywhere when it's hot, as dogs like to do. Cats are also better at finding cool places to get away from the heat. Personally, I don't think cats benefit as much as dogs do from being shaved in the summer. But if it makes your life easier, go ahead. Just make sure to find a groomer who can do it in a gentle way.

### CLEANING EARS

Make it as comfortable for the cat as possible. Instead of making a production out of it, gently massage the cat's ears with your fingers. When he is comfortable with this, wrap some gauze around your finger and dip it in ear-cleaning solution. Massage his ear with one hand, and use the other hand to clean it. The cat won't even realize he is getting his ears cleaned.

## Why do we need to groom cats since they groom themselves all day long?

In nature, cats don't shed as much as they do indoors. When cats lived outdoors, they shed mostly in the spring and fall. They also ate a more natural diet of live game. Indoor cats are often fed a kibble diet and exposed to no variations in season. As a result, they shed more year-round. Even though the cat licks himself, he still needs help. If we don't brush the cat, his fur will be all over the furniture and clothes or in the cat's stomach. It won't stay there very long, because he will vomit it up into our shoes in the middle of the night.

## How do I get rid of my cat's ear mites? They always seem to come back.

Ear mites are arachnids related to spiders. They are almost microscopic and live in the cat's ears, sucking the blood through the thin skin. Since the skin is thinner in the cat's ears, it is easier for the mites to access the cat's blood supply. The black gunk you find in the cat's ears is digested blood secreted by the mites. In the past, the common treatment was to clean out the cat's ears with mineral oil, which would smother the mites. Nowadays, there are more effective prescription medications. The problem is that they must be used for a long, long, long time. Mites multiply exponentially. In other words, if you kill all of the mites but one, the next day there will be two, then four, then eight, and so on. Most people medication until it appears that the mites are gone—but they are not really gone. One or two are still lurking, so the problem starts all over again. You need to keep using the medication long after you think the mites are gone.

## How often does my cat need a bath?

Bathe your cat whenever he is dirty. If you ask the cat, he will probably say that he never needs a bath. But cats can be bathed the same way that dogs can. When you bathe a cat, it should be in a gentle, nonconfrontational way. Some cats can be bathed in the sink, but they must have secure footing. Put the cat in the sink, wet him with warm water with the dish sprayer, use cat shampoo, and rinse.

Many cats will tolerate this just fine. However, some don't like the feel of running water. For those cats, I have success using a three-bucket method. The first bucket is filled with warm water and soap, and the other two contain clean rinse water. Lower the cat into the first bucket with his head and front paws hanging over the side. The warm water seems to mesmerize the cat. Maintain gentle pressure on the top of his head to keep him in the bucket of warm soapy water while you gently massage the soap through his coat. When he is clean, lift him out and lower him into the second bucket, which contains rinse water, and then repeat this step with the third bucket to ensure that his coat is thoroughly rinsed. Carefully lift him out and wrap him in a towel. Dry him as best as you can, then let him run under the bed, lick himself dry, and sulk for a while.

This method works for many uncooperative cats, but every cat is an individual. If you try to lower your cat into the bucket and he fights you, don't push the issue; you will lose. In that case, take the cat to a groomer and have him bathed professionally. Either way, if your cat needs a bath, there is no reason to avoid doing it.

> ### TRIMMING TIPS
> The easiest way to trim a cat's nails is by wrapping the cat in a big blanket like a baby. Pull one paw out at a time and clip the nails. If you don't think your cat will tolerate this, don't try, because you are going to get hurt. Pound for pound, cats are much stronger than people. Take the cat to a groomer or vet who can clip nails without causing harm to either party.

## My cat grooms herself all day long, and she is starting to look bald. Is this possible, or is it my imagination?

When I was a kid, cats were outdoors all day, climbing trees, chasing squirrels, and running away from packs of dogs. They never had time to excessively groom themselves the way that many house cats do today. Many cats that are kept indoors have very little to do and will compensate by excessively grooming themselves the same way that dogs would chew their paws or horses would crib on a stall or a bird would pluck its feathers out.

If your cat has gotten into an excessive grooming habit, he needs to have his day broken up with more activities. This can be accomplished by giving him more frequent small meals, more interactive toys, or a window perch so he can look out, preferably at a bird feeder set up in front of the window. You can also find videos made for cats that show birds feeding at a bird feeder. Many things will work, but you need to find a way to keep your cat busy and occupied during the day. This excessive grooming may also indicate a medical problem, so be sure to consult your vet as well.

## Do deshedding tools really cut down on grooming time? How about deshedding treats and supplements?

Any physical interaction with the cat's hair, whether it's your fingers, a piece of duct tape wrapped around your hand, a brush, a comb, or a deshedding tool, will remove shed fur and cut down on the amount of cat hair in your house. Some items and tools remove more hair than others do, but the goal is to remove as much of the loose fur as possible so that it's not all over your furniture or ingested by the cat.

Diet is the most important factor as far as maintaining a cat's coat in top condition. Years ago, cats shed very little in our homes because the cats were outside for most of the day, which also gave them opportunities to supplement their diets with small birds, rodents, and lizards that they caught. These cats were also exposed to natural photoperiods of the seasons. They shed a little more in the spring and fall, less in the summer and winter. Regular exposure to grass and underbrush also helped remove a good amount of loose coat before the cat came back into the house.

In contrast, today many cats live indoors and are exclusively fed processed commercial diets. They are not exposed to natural photoperiods or temperature changes, which also causes them to shed more. It's best to minimize shedding by feeding a better quality canned, homemade, or raw diet.

## What is the best way to prevent fleas?

Fleas are always a problem for cats, mainly because it is not easy to apply dips or flea sprays to uncooperative animals. When a cat has fleas, the fleas really like to hide in the short fur on the bridge of the cat's nose and forehead. It's amazing how many fleas can hide in that short fur. To get flea spray into this fur, you need to put it on a sponge and saturate the areas thoroughly. However, new products like Advantage and Frontline are much easier to use. Applying a few drops to the skin on the cat's back will take care of all the fleas. I am not a big fan of technology, but this is one technological advance that I consider a really good value. Never use a dog product on a cat, and read the directions and weight requirements on all flea products. Certain insecticides, such as permethrin, can be toxic, even fatal, to cats.

### WHO SHEDS THE MOST?

All cats shed the same amount, but when a longhair cat sheds, the fur generally remains stuck in his coat until the cat is brushed and combed. When the fur falls out of a short-hair cat, it lands on our clothes and furniture, but the frequency with which the fur falls out is the same. Fur shed from a shorthair cat may be more noticeable, but it's not going to result in the massive mats and knots that you will see on a longhair cat that is not groomed regularly.

## Frosty: The Cat Who Loved Going for Walks

It is hard to train a cat to walk with you on a leash like a dog does because it's usually not in the cat's nature to do this. However, there are a few exceptions to this rule. One of my favorite cats was a big tabby named Frosty who walked into my life when I was about ten years old. He was a big, grizzled, unneutered tom, covered with battle scars and with a tick about the size of a grapefruit hanging over one eye. He strolled into our back-yard, sat down in one of the lawn chairs, and claimed the whole territory. All of my other cats would run in horror from him. But he had the most personality of any cat I've ever known.

There was a golf course across the street from my house, and early in the morning I would sneak my dogs over there to go for a long run. Frosty became very bonded to me and my dogs. In no time at all, he decided to start coming with us on our morn-ing walk to the golf course. It soon became the daily routine for Frosty, the dogs, and I to take our morning walk. Frosty never wore a leash. He walked with us simply because he enjoyed it. Such is the nature of cats and part of why they fascinate me.

But the days of cats wandering freely are over. In this day and age, a loose cat will be hit by a car. Cats also do much damage to songbirds and native rodent populations. Pet cats destroy thousands of native songbirds, an issue I'll address later in this book. Not all cats will walk with you like Frosty did, but if you get your cat accustomed to a harness and leash, he can enjoy the outdoors while being kind to the environment!

### WALK THIS WAY

The easiest way to teach a cat to walk next to you on a leash is by using a bit of baby food on a spoon. Glue a plastic spoon to a long, thin dowel. Put a bit of baby food on the spoon and hold the dowel at the cat's eye level. Use this to lure the cat along with you as you walk. Trainers call this a target stick. In time, instead of having the target stick in front of the cat all the time, offer it at the end of the walk as a reward.

## Why do so many people think that cats cannot be trained? Are they really that hard to train?

Anyone who has seen cats in movies or in television shows such as *Sabrina the Teenage Witch* knows how well cats can be trained. The problem is that animals respond to rewards in different ways. For a dog, a reward is either food or praise and attention. If a dog happens to value food more than praise and attention, he may sometimes be labeled difficult.

However, in reality that individual dog's salary requirements were never negotiated. The same thing applies to cats.

Cats have a very high opinion of themselves, and they prefer a salary that rarely includes praise. Cats mainly respond to food rewards. Note how quickly your cat races through the house when he hears the sound of the can opener. Now, if we combined a command such as *Come on, kitty* with the sound of the can opener, eventually the cat would realize that *Come on, kitty* means that it's dinnertime. This is exactly how clicker training works: the cat learns to associate a particular sound with a particular reward and a particular behavior.

Any cat can be trained to do anything, from walking on a leash to jumping on your shoulder to picking up objects, but you need to use an effective reward combined with a training routine that the cat can understand.

That's why clicker training is the best method for cats. It's a bit involved to explain in this short paragraph, but there are numerous books and Internet resources that you can consult for more information.

## Can you train a cat to do tricks the way you can train a dog?

Cats, dogs, killer whales—all animals, for that matter—learn in the same manner. Cats can be trained to do the same behaviors as dogs do. I have taught them to walk at heel, come on command, and jump on my shoulder. Actually, cats can do more tricks than dogs can because they have more physical dexterity. They can do things like climbing walls, turning doorknobs, and closing window shades because they can manipulate their paws more nimbly than dogs can.

The perfect example of what a cat can be trained to do can be seen in the Disney movie *Homeward Bound: The Incredible Journey*. There is a scene where the two dogs are in a dog pound. The Himalayan cat was trained to climb onto their cages and unlock them. If you look closely, you can clearly see the cat eating a bit of food that the trainer placed on the cage latches. A dog couldn't be trained to do this because he would not be able to climb up a wire or open a latch with his paws.

## I've seen people walk cats on leashes like they walk dogs. How can I train my kitty to do this?

Cats can be trained to tolerate a leash very easily. Get the right harness and leash. A step-in harness works best. The cat puts one paw through each side, and it clips over the back. The key is to let the cat get used to wearing this in the house for a day. Once he is used to wearing the harness, attach a very light leash and just sit there watching TV with the cat on the leash. When the cat accepts both the leash and harness, open the door and sit on the step or porch with the cat on the leash. Allow the cat to look outside and feel comfortable going in and out. Gradually increase your forays outside with the cat. In no time at all, he will feel fine wearing the leash and harness outside.

## How can I get my cat to stop tearing up my rugs? I bought her a scratching post, but she won't use it—why?

Cats do what they want, when they want to do it. From the cat's point of view, both rugs and scratching posts are simply part of her environment. She will choose the one that works best for scratching. If the cat is using the rug, that's because the scratching post is not as secure or doesn't do as good a job on the cat's nails. You have to make the scratching post more desirable for the cat. Most of the scratching posts people buy are too small and too flimsy. The cat needs to be able to stretch out and pull against the post with no resistance. If it rocks back and forth or seems unstable, the cat won't use it. In nature, cats use trees, so you may need a bigger scratching post. In our house, we use 5-foot tall posts with shelves and hideaways, all covered with sisal rope and secure Berber carpeting. We scent it with catnip, so it smells really good to the cat.

You also need to make the cat's chosen scratching area less appealing. To discourage cats from scratching furniture, apply strips of double-sided tape to the edges of couches and chairs. The cat's paws will stick to the tape, and she won't like it. For rugs and floors, buy a roll of plastic carpet runner. Cut it into pieces, turn the pieces upside down so that the little bumps are on the outside, and place them wherever you don't want the cat scratching. If it's a rug, place an appropriate-sized piece on the rug. Drape a piece over the back of the couch to stop the cat from scratching there. The plastic will make these areas unattractive for the cat, so she will choose to use the scratching post. The secret is tricking the cat into making your idea her idea, but none of this will work unless the scratching post is a viable alternative for the cat.

## How do I get my cat to stop playing in his water bowl?

The idea that cats have an aversion to water is an old wives' tale. Some cats don't like water; some do. I've mentioned that some cats, like the Turkish Van breed, positively love water. Many cats like to play in it. The key is to make the water dish as small as possible so the cat has less water to splash around in.

A small ceramic dish will usually work just right. I've also found that it helps to place a bowl of shiny glass marbles next to the cat's water dish. The cat will enjoy putting her paw in the marbles and swishing them around like a bowl of water, thus distracting him from the water bowl. Be sure not to use cat's eye marbles, or your cat may get offended!

Snowflake always sleeps with me at night; she seems to have naturally accustomed herself to a human schedule. My new cat, Thomas, however, is bouncing off the walls at 4 a.m., and if he has access to the bedroom, he will try to entreat us to join him. I have no problem kicking Thomas out, but I feel bad confining Snowflake to the bedroom. Is there any way I can get him to be less nocturnal?

Cats are nocturnal. That's a basic fact, although older cats tend to sleep all night and stay awake during the day. Since this is a new cat, I assume he is a young cat, and it's normal for kittens to bounce around the house like crazy all night. This became very apparent to me when my wife and I first got married and we were living in a studio apartment. There was no way to stop the young cats from bouncing all over the walls all night. I ended up locking them in the bathroom at night with a litter box, a bed, and some toys. The first few nights, they yowled and threw themselves against the door. But after that, they accepted it. After they were a year old, their nocturnal gymnastics stopped, and we let them sleep in the same room with us.

If you don't want the cat bouncing around your room at 4 a.m., the cat shouldn't be in your room at 4 a.m. Keep the door closed. However, since your other cat is sleeping with you at night, you have to keep a litter box in the bedroom for that cat to use and another box outside the bedroom for the other cat to use.

## How can I train my cat not to sleep on the stove?

Your cat is sleeping on the stove because it's a nice place to sleep. If you could watch him 24/7, you could take him off the stove every time he jumped up there. He would soon decide that the stove wasn't such a nice place to sleep because he was always disturbed when he tried to sleep there. The best way to make a stove unappealing for a cat is to put tin foil on it. If the cat was sleeping on a countertop, you could put strips of double-stick tape on it, which cats also dislike. But tape would leave sticky residue all over the stove.

When you are not using the stove, place some sheets of aluminum foil on the top. Cats typically dislike lying on crinkly, shiny tin foil. The foil will make the surface unpleasant without damaging the stove.

## Selective Cat Breeding

Looking through a copy of *All Pets* magazine from 1953, I noticed that the only breeds of cats advertised were Burmese, Siamese, Persian, Manx, and Abyssinian. Nowadays, if you visit a cat show, you will find at least thirty or forty different breeds. Where did so many breeds come from?

More than anything, this increase in the number of breeds was a result of change in perception about cats. People really didn't selectively breed cats before the 1950s. Cats lived outdoors, they were almost never neutered, and breeding was never supervised. There was no selective breeding done in those days. Any mutations that might have occurred would have probably been considered as defects, and the kitten could have been drowned—even a mutation as simple as folded ears would have been looked at in horror by most people.

When I was a kid, I worked at a garden center. There were plenty of stray cats around, and every now and then we would discover a litter of kittens behind a bag of fertilizer or something. We could have easily put those kittens in a box and found homes for them. But the owner of the garden center, a man who was a kind father, a wonderful husband, and a good businessman, thought nothing of drowning these poor little kittens. And this was not unheard of. Some people simply drove their unwanted cat a few miles away from their house and released it.

It wasn't until the late 1950s that America saw a large-scale commitment to cat breeding and care. Cat breeders take great pains to control every aspect of their chosen breed. Mutations are no longer regarded as freaks of nature. They are seen as valuable genetic variations, and ideal specimens are valued and admired.

## I've had many purring cats in my life, but my latest cat prefers to chirp like a bird all day long. What does it mean?

My Russian cat, Nastia, chirps, and I've seen many Ragdoll cats and Maine Coon cats who do this also. It seems to be genetic. Wild cats like cheetahs, cougars, and servals make very odd sounds. The meow is something unique to domestic cats. Chirping and chuffing is natural for wild cats, and many domestic cats retain this behavior. We expect mountain lions to growl and scream because this is how they are portrayed on nature shows.

You may not realize it, but these sounds are usually dubbed in. When you meet a cougar in person, it makes a chirping noise, which is not something you would expect from such a large, powerful animal.

### IN THE DARK
Ophthalmologists agree that all cats can see in the dark better than dogs can. But dogs still see pretty well in the dark, well enough to get around better than we do.

## Why do my cat's eyes glow in the dark?

Cats' eyes have a reflective layer of tissue called the tapetum lucidum, which magnifies incoming light. This layer also produces the characteristic greenish glow.

## Why do cats have whiskers? When my cat loses a whisker, will it grow back? Does it hurt if I cut my cat's whiskers?

The technical name for whiskers is *vibrissae*. The longest ones are found on the cat's muzzle and above the eyes. Another set is found on the back of the cat's front wrists. These hairs are sensitive to air currents and provide sensory information to the cat. The whiskers also help protect the cat's nose and eyes. The whiskers around the eyes are especially important because stimulating them triggers the blink reflex. As to whether or not it will hurt the cat to cut his whiskers, anything that sensitive would be sensitive to pain. Don't do it. But whiskers do fall out and grow back on their own.

## Are curly-coated cats hypoallergenic?

Curly-coated cats like the Devon Rex and Cornish Rex do not shed very much, but they are not hypoallergenic. The Selkirk Rex, LaPerms, and American

Wirehair are also curly coated and carry this mutation. If an allergist has confirmed that you are allergic to cats, you will be allergic to all cats—including rex cats—unless you get allergy shots. The rex mutation is seen in dogs, rabbits, guinea pigs, and cats. It causes the fur to be short and wiry because it lacks the outer guard hairs. Because of their short coats, rex cats do not shed very much, but they also have reduced tolerance for cold weather.

Many people ask me to recommend a nonallergenic breed of cat. The problem is that cat allergies have nothing to do with the cat's fur. The allergens come from the protein, oils, and dander from the cat's skin and from its saliva. The cat licks himself all over, and he comes in contact with surfaces throughout your house. Bits of dander and protein will be deposited throughout the house. When they dry, they become airborne and irritate the mucous membranes of anyone

## Hybrid Cats

Back in the 1970s, I participated in a breeding experiment in which Asian Leopard cats were crossed with domestic Abyssinian cats. The first-generation hybrids were complete lunatics. They were even wilder than the Asian Leopard cat sire. However, a domestic nature came out in subsequent generations of this breeding experiment. As a general rule, after four generations of hybrid breeding away from the original wild cross, the cats can be considered domestic. And these were as safe and friendly as any other cat.

Breeders of Bengal cats today have outdone themselves. They really have produced a cat with the look of a wild animal and the behavior of a domestic cat. In fact, the Bengal cat looks so wild that if you plan to export one, the government has to issue a CITES permit (CITES stands for the Convention on International Trade in Endangered Species of Wild Fauna and Flora) for that cat to prevent illegal animal dealers from exporting wild spotted cats under the guise of domestically bred Bengals. Because today's domestic Bengals look so exotic, people had been using them as cover to illegally export real wild cats.

I take my hat off to all of the Bengal breeders out there. I've had many wild cats in my life. They are illegal to keep as pets, and they don't make good ones—I have the scars to prove it. Those desiring that exotic look can satisfy themselves by getting a Bengal.

with an allergic sensitivity to cats. Even a hairless cat like the Sphynx can trigger an allergic reaction.

One breed, the Siberian, produces less dander and allergy-inducing proteins than other cat breeds. But this is unrelated to the length or type of coat. It is claimed that the Norwegian Forest Cat can be tolerated by allergy sufferers. As far as I know, there have been no research studies to confirm this anecdotal evidence.

## Is it true that Persians can't jump fences?

Persian cats have shorter legs and heavier bodies than most cats do, but they can still jump many times their height. I have seen Persians easily go over a 6-foot fence. And a Persian cat can definitely run faster than people can.

## What is the Munchkin cat? Is this really a breed?

Munchkin cats have the same genetic trait that causes short legs in dog breeds like Dachshunds. This trait has been selectively bred into the Munchkin. What is interesting is the double standard that sometimes applies to this breed. Some people feel it is cruel to perpetuate this trait in a breed of cat, yet no one has problems accepting the same trait in a Dachshund or short-legged terrier—or any dog breed with short legs and a long body.

Many traits in domesticated animals are a result of intentionally manipulating spontaneously occurring mutations. At this point, very few dogs resemble their wolf ancestor. Now, cats have been domesticated for less than 10,000 years, compared with 12,000 years of breeding domesticated dogs. Most of the cat breeds known today have been developed starting in the mid-twentieth century. We began to notice and selectively breed various mutations in cats. I am sure that folded ears, no tails, and short legs had cropped up in the past, but the usual response was not to value these traits by introducing a new exotic breed.

If this is OK for dogs, why not cats? The late, great Roger Caras used to speculate whether cat domestication would eventually catch up to that of dogs. Look at the size variation normally found in dogs. Maybe in 200 years we will have domestic cats weighing 50 or 60 pounds. Now that we are crossing servals with domestic cats to create 30-pound hybrids, Roger's prediction may well come true. However, most people have trouble controlling a 10-pound cat, and I can't imagine what they would do with a 50-pound cat.

## What is a Savannah cat?

In the same way that breeders derived the Bengal cat from a hybridization experiment between domestic cats and Asian Leopard cats (*Felis bengal*), cat breeders realized that you could cross a domestic cat with the serval, which is a long-legged, medium-sized cat that resembles a small cheetah and is native to Africa. These matings are always done with a male domestic cat and a female serval. This is because the gestation period of the serval is longer than

that of the domestic cat. A domestic queen would not be able to carry hybrid kittens to full term, but a serval can. Not all of these hybrid kittens are fertile, and serval litters rarely contain more than two kittens, so these hybrids are few and far between, making them extremely expensive pets. These large exotic pets are not legal to keep in every state and jurisdiction. Here in my state, New York, it is not legal to keep them as pets. People in other states have found Savannah cats to be affectionate, gentle, and intelligent companions. As with Bengals, four generations removed from the foundation (the mating of wild to domestic cat) produce a pet as domesticated as any other house cat. Over the years, I have kept many wild animals as pets, mainly to learn the differences between wild and domestic animals. I have only been able to do this because I was able to obtain the necessary state and federal permits, and no animal is worth of all that paperwork!

## Is it true that Ragdoll cats don't feel pain?

That's an old wives' tale based on the fact that Ragdoll cats are so easygoing (the name comes from the fact that they like to lie around like rag dolls). The

story goes that they were genetically engineered in a laboratory to be used for experiments. However, this is just a story.

Ragdolls are limp and relaxed when you hold them in your arms. They drape themselves over your arm and hang there. But they feel pain as much as any other cat does. Their nature is just a temperament trait. I'm friends with a famous Ragdoll cat breeder, and I use a lot of her Ragdolls on TV because they are so easy to work with.

## Why do Siamese cats look so different from all other cats?

The mutation that causes the coloration of the Siamese cat is confined to areas of the body with a higher body temperature. The ears, face, legs, and tail, which are farther from the body's core, are cooler and have darker pigment. This particular mutation is found not only in cats but in Himalayan rabbits and now fancy rats as well. It has been introduced into other cat breeds such as the Ragdoll, and Himalayan cats are a product of introducing the Siamese genes into the Persian breed. The same mutation causes cooler parts of the body to be darker in color in all these breeds and the eyes to be blue.

## Why are Siamese cats so noisy?

This is a breed characteristic. Most likely Siamese cats were noisy before they became a separate breed. The same gene causes the Siamese color pattern in Persian cats and Ragdoll cats, and they aren't noisy at all. Ragdolls are one of the quietest breeds. Most likely, the native cats of Thailand were noisy originally. One theory is that this ancient breed could be more vocal because of their long history with humans. Intelligent and perceptive, Siamese seem to understand that humans communicate mainly by vocalizing, and so they've learned to become vocal too. Once the gene for the dark points and blue eyes occurred in those cats, people liked it and perpetuated it. So, you had noisy cats with light bodies, contrasting points, and blue eyes. But the noisy nature came first.

## Why can you show neutered cats in cat shows but you can't show neutered dogs in dog shows?

That determination is made by the Cat Fanciers Association. Clubs that sponsor cat shows decide what classes to offer. They have the option of offering classes for altered cats, but the AKC has not given dog clubs this option at this point; they may do so in the future.

## Which is the oldest domesticated cat breed?

Most people consider the Persian, Abyssinian, and Siamese to be the oldest recognized breeds, although spotted cats appear in ancient Egyptian art and are believed to be the ancestors of the Egyptian Mau, also an ancient breed.

started playing with these kittens, and they became acclimated to humans. The friendliest cats were probably kept for breeding. This could also have happened with other wild cats in other parts of the world. Food would have provided the most likely motivation for a cat to hang around a human settlement.

## Do Scottish Folds hear as well as other cats?

That would be like asking if Bloodhounds can hear as well as German Shepherds do, or if lop-eared rabbits can hear as well as other rabbits can. It always seemed to me that dropped ears would compromise hearing, but veterinary specialists have assured me that they can hear just as well.

## Where did the whole "nine lives" thing originate?

I really can't say for sure since I am not a historian. Most likely this stemmed from people regularly witnessing incidents that demonstrated the cat's durability. Outwardly, cats appear to be very resilient. Actually, they are not as resilient as we think they are. They are very good at hiding their feelings and symptoms. For instance, a cat might fall from a height, land on his feet, and run away. Anyone seeing this would think that the cat was virtually immortal. That cat may have subsequently crawled off under a bush and died—but no one saw this. As a result, it was believed that cats were indestructible.

I really can't say how the idea of nine lives came about. I can see everyone getting a second chance, but not nine chances. If anyone has the answer, please let me know.

## Peppermint: The Cat Who Taught Me About Natural History

When I was a kid, I had a wonderful black cat with one eye named Peppermint. As was the custom at the time, all of the cats were outdoors every day. Peppermint was an amazing hunter. He always brought home birds and small mammals. Whenever I discovered Peppermint with a small animal in his mouth, I would pry his jaws apart in spite of his growling and snarling. Some of these small creatures were not harmed, and I would keep them in aquariums or terrariums and study them.

As a result, I learned a lot about small native rodents that you would normally never see. For instance, Peppermint caught a lot of shrews, small insectivores that are rarely seen and rarely studied because of their secretive nature. But as a child, I had many shrews. I fed them earthworms and insects and learned about their behavior. I also kept meadow voles, white-footed deer mice, and chipmunks. I was always fascinated with the natural world, and Peppermint provided access to it. I learned things that I could never find in a book.

One time, Peppermint brought home a white-footed deer mouse. I put her in a cage, and three days later she had a litter of babies. I released the mother, and the babies grew up and became quite friendly. I had my own population of tame white-footed deer mice, and I learned a great deal about rare small rodents. Peppermint also used to catch moles all the time. I was one of the few people to successfully keep moles in captivity. I even had a rare star-nosed mole, which would not have been possible without Peppermint. I sure wasn't going to find a mole at the local pet store. Peppermint also brought home many ground-nesting birds, such as song sparrows and bobwhite quail, and I learned a great deal about them by keeping the survivors.

Looking back, I realize that Peppermint opened up a world of natural history for me. Of course, the number of animals that I successfully rescued from Peppermint was a very small percentage of his total catch. He killed far more.

Not knowing any better, I used to put a bell on him to try and prevent him from hunting small birds and animals. But it made no difference. The only useful purpose in putting a bell on a cat is to allow you to know where your cat is. At night, I would call him to come in. I would open the back door and scream his name as loudly as I could. Eventually, I would hear his bell faintly ringing as he made his way home for the night. The ringing would get louder and louder. Out of the darkness, Peppermint would appear at my feet, and I would bring him in and feed him.

Thanks to Peppermint and cats like him, the area where I grew up is now devoid of shrews, moles, and deer mice. From personal experience, I know exactly how much damage cats can do to wildlife. Peppermint was wearing a bell and he was very well fed, yet he wreaked havoc on the native populations.

Is it a good idea to get veterinary insurance, or is it just a scam to play on my sense of guilt and get my money? Kitty's health bills can add up, but is it really worthwhile to pay a premium each month?

This depends on your insurance policy. Nowadays, there are many insurance policies available for pets, and, just like human insurance policies, some are better than others. In this respect, I would recommend looking at the individual policies and deciding for yourself.

I have health insurance for all my pets, and it has saved me financially many times. I recommend it to anyone who can afford it. Do an Internet search for pet health insurance policies, and find one that suits your style.

I've heard over and over again how inhumane it is to declaw a cat. Isn't there any circumstance in which it is justified? What if it's either declaw the cat or get rid of him?

Declawing cats is a very hot topic, and people tend to become quite emotional when discussing this. I personally find declawing yucky. I don't like the idea of removing each toe at the first joint. But I am not comfortable with any kind of surgical alteration of animals. I don't like to trim bird's wings, dock puppies' tails, or crop puppies' ears. Nor have I ever found it necessary. But it is perfectly legal to do these things in the United States. And the fact that I don't care for it doesn't mean that I have the right to judge anyone who does it.

Declawing is a much more complicated surgical procedure than most people realize. The veterinarian must cut through the bone of the first joint of each toe. This is a surgical amputation of the tip of each toe, which must be done under full anesthesia by an experienced vet. I've known people to shop around for better prices on this procedure only to discover that their cat's leg was paralyzed for a few days after surgery. This can happen if the vet puts a tourniquet high on the leg instead of tying off each toe.

Now what happens when the cat wakes up from the anesthesia and discovers that he has no claws? In my experience, nothing happens. The cat functions just as he always did. I have known many wild and domestic cats that were declawed, and they seem to do just fine and don't miss their claws at all. I think the cats that miss their claws the most are those kept in the company of other cats that aren't declawed. In that case, the cat may feel defenseless when confronted by another cat.

I've only noticed a difference in one particular cat that tended to bite more after he was declawed. I guess this cat realized that his claws no longer produced the same results.

When I was a kid, my neighbor had a Siamese cat that had his front paws declawed, and I saw that cat go right up trees as if he had claws on all four feet. I have never declawed any of my cats, and my house is full of lovely Victorian furniture that I'm not allowed to sit on. We have always been able

## Fido

Many years ago, someone gave me a front-declawed calico cat named Fido. She was the toughest cat I ever owned. No dog, cat, orangutan, mongoose, or anything else could stand up to Fido. She was a tough, determined cat, declawed or not. She wouldn't hesitate to beat up any animal she chose. At the time, I also had a baboon named Georgette who hated cats. One day, Georgette got out of her cage, rushed over to Fido, picked her up, and was about to bite her head off. Fido turned, sunk her teeth into Georgette's hand, and attempted to disembowel Georgette with her back feet, which still had claws. It was definitely a lovely moment in pet keeping.

Georgette dropped Fido, screamed in agony, and ran to her cage, sucking on her wounded hand. Even without claws, Fido was able to beat up a baboon. She was also able to catch mice and scratch people. She would sit on the floor at the front of my store, looking cute. When a child came up to pet her, she would whack them across the face with her paw, causing a scratch. We could never figure out how she managed to do this. Fido was about fifteen when she took up this hobby, and the pads on her front paws were very rough. Most likely, this was enough to cause a scratch.

to train them to use scratching posts. Through the judicious use of scat mats, catnip, and cat-repellent spray, my wife has been able to trick them into thinking that their cat trees and scratching posts are much better than our furniture. If you don't have the time or inclination to persuade your cat not to claw your furniture, and your vet can safely declaw the cat's front paws, that is your choice.

Obviously, declawing is not the horror that some people paint it to be. Even the late, great Roger Caras owned a Siamese cat that was declawed. The cat was so mean to his other cats, he had no choice but to have the cat declawed. If I were a cat and my owner couldn't train me properly to use the scratching post and I had the option of either getting declawed and living in a nice house or keeping my claws and going to an animal shelter, I would opt to stay in the nice house. Now, some people find fault with the owner who opts to take his cat to a shelter because the cat clawed the furniture, but this isn't always a straightforward decision. When I was a kid, one of my cats clawed up my father's leather dining room chairs. He promptly took that cat for a ride. If I'd had the money and known a vet who could do it, I would have had that cat declawed so I could keep him. Declawing a cat is really a pragmatic choice rather than a moral choice, and it should be viewed as such.

## I keep seeing ads for soft claws and other plastic sheaths to place over my cat's nails. Do these really work? Is it hard to get them on the cat? It seems that a cat would be able to get them off in seconds if he wanted to.

They actually do work very well. They are applied with a little glue. Some cats are more accepting of them than others are. This depends on the individual cat's temperament and your ability to handle the cat. It will be much easier if you have trained your cat to allow you to handle his paws and push his claws out of their sheaths to be trimmed or filed. A cat like this probably won't object to having the soft claws applied. They can be a great alternative if you don't have the time to train your cat to not scratch the furniture or to use a scratching post.

## My mother says it's cruel to keep a cat indoors. When she was growing up, all of her cats were allowed outside. Is it safe to leave my cat outside when I am at work?

When I was a kid, all of my cats were allowed to run around outside. And they were hit by cars, were chased by dogs, were killed by foxes and coyotes, and suffered from giant abscesses from getting into fights with other cats. They had much shorter lives than cats do today. They used up their nine lives really quickly.

Given a choice, if cats were aware of the dangers they faced outdoors, I am sure they would voluntarily choose to stay indoors. But animals cannot predict the future or decide what is in their best interests. So it is your responsibility to keep your cat indoors, where he will have a much safer life. It's also your responsibility to ensure that your cat's life is no less enriched and interactive than it would be if he did go outside.

Our other obligation as pet keepers is to safeguard the wildlife in our backyards. The mice that cats are killing outdoors are not the house mice that cause damage in our barns and homes. These cats are killing white-footed deer mice, meadow voles, and chipmunks, which are all crucial food sources for our birds of prey such as barn owls, American kestrels, and screech owls. Because of outdoor cats, these birds are deprived of their food sources. Then we wonder why we see so few of these bird species.

Keeping your cat indoors is a win-win situation. The cat lives longer, and the wildlife lives longer.

## What do I do if my cat runs away?

If you lose your cat, it's pretty useless to go outside and call him. If he is scared, he won't want to be found, and you will not find him. The best thing is to let

everyone know that your cat is missing and offer a big reward for his return. Once he becomes sufficiently lonely and hungry, he will want to be found. Until then, you are not going to find him.

Years ago, I had a female black cat named Magic. She was a feral cat that I had brought into the house. She hated it indoors and tried to escape at every opportunity. One day, she managed to sneak out and was gone. Eight days went by with no sign of her despite our canvassing and searching. On the eighth day, my dear mother-in-law walked into my store,

LOST CAT

PLEASE CALL 555-1857!

grabbed me by the hand, and asked me to come to her car immediately. On the front seat lay Magic, dehydrated and just skin and bones. Apparently, my mother-in-law was driving past our house and saw Magic lying on the front steps. She picked her up and brought her right to me. She was so dehydrated that the vet could hardly find a vein to start an IV. She did recover, but she

## Beeper: the Bird Who Came to Lunch

I've worked with Martha Stewart for more than ten years. In the process, I've had many encounters with her pets. One day, about nine years ago, I was at her home in Westport, Connecticut. At the time, she had eight Himalayan cats. Martha has also bred canaries for many years, and she has quite a few. On this occasion, I went there to do a photo shoot with Martha and some of my tame canaries. The photo shoot was about Martha standing in front of one of her aviaries with one of my tame canaries named Beeper sitting on her finger.

A photographer was waiting at her house. I had Beeper in a little cage. In her kitchen, I took him out of the cage, and he perched on my finger just as her phone rang. Of course, this was an important business call that was going to take quite some time. So I went to sit in the living room with Beeper on my finger. Out of nowhere, two cats suddenly appeared and proceeded to glare at poor Beeper perched on my finger. I didn't want to disturb Martha by going back into the kitchen for his cage, so I tiptoed into the dining room, and Beeper and I started reading a copy of *Martha Stewart Living*. Again, out of nowhere, a cat jumped on the dining room table with his hungry eyes riveted on poor little Beeper.

At that point, I thought, *This is ridiculous*. Was there anyplace in this house that was safe from cats? So we went into the bathroom, closed the door, and leaned against the wall and read the magazine. The area around the sink was covered by a curtain, and in no time at all, out came a cat from under the curtain. He jumped onto the toilet, looked at Beeper, and started licking his chops. I decided that the only safe place for this poor little bird was outdoors. I ran out the back door, and Beeper and I spent the rest of the hour strolling in Martha's garden until she was finally off the phone and we could get on with the photo shoot.

Beeper is still alive today. Ancient and arthritic, he has no idea how close he came to being lunch for Martha Stewart's cats.

was never quite the same. I think she suffered some kind of permanent brain damage from the trauma. Needless to say, she never again tried to run away. I think she was accidentally locked in someone's shed or garage for a week. Like poor Lassie, once she was able to get out, she struggled to get home and collapsed.

Losing your cat and getting him back involves a lot of luck. Losing him is bad luck, but you hope that you will have good luck and be reunited. If Magic had not gotten out of her prison in time and my mother-in-law had not seen her, she would not have survived.

## Is there any type of fencing that can keep a cat from leaving your yard?

Yes, there is. Cats can climb just about any fence. But lions, tigers, and jaguars can also climb fences, and many of these animals are kept in open-topped enclosures in zoos and wild animal parks. The key is to keep some type of baffle at the top of the fence. When the cat climbs to the top, he confronts a baffle that extends at a right angle to the fence, and he is forced to climb down.

Nowadays, many companies specialize in cat-proof fencing; you can find one by searching online. Such a fence will allow your cat to go out and enjoy your backyard in the daytime when there are fewer opportunities for him to hunt birds and small animals. Just be sure to bring him indoors at night so he cannot wreak havoc on the native wildlife.

## How long could my cat last in the wild, and would he eventually "go feral"?

A cat will not become feral once he has been socialized. A house cat in the wild would become a stray, but not feral. Some cats, such as the Ragdoll breed, are too docile to survive in the wild.

## What is the best way to stop my cat from killing the birds at my birdfeeder?

The only way to prevent a cat from killing birds at a birdfeeder is to prevent any access to the birds. And the only way to do this is by keeping the cat indoors. It's an old wives' tale that keeping a bell on the cat will warn the birds of the cat's approach. First of all, how are the birds supposed to know that a ringing bell means that a cat is approaching? The world is full of bells, whistles, and sirens, and birds ignore all of these routinely. Second, even if the birds did manage to make this connection, it wouldn't be much of a warning. A cat stalks feeding birds so slowly and stealthily that the bell would not ring until the cat makes his final dash, and it's too late for the bird to fly away by then.

## My house is overrun with mice, and my cat seems to have no interest in helping to get rid of them. How can I convince her to hunt the mice?

Well, you really can't convince her to hunt the mice. Cats have been domesticated for thousands of years. As a result, many of them have lost their predatory instinct. Although this is an ancestral instinct, it doesn't remain equally strong in every cat. You can see this in many of the cats I bring on TV with me.

Your cat has no desire to hunt mice because she doesn't recognize mice as a food source. If you need a cat that will hunt house mice, you may need to get another cat that has a stronger natural predatory instinct. But you also need to understand something about mice. If you see one, there are probably ten more that you didn't see. So for every one that the cat catches, there are probably ten more happily running around that managed to evade the cat. The only way to really get rid of a mouse problem is to prevent them from getting into the house and to make sure that they have no access to food. Mice have survived in a world full of predators for eons. The mere fact that there is a cat in the house doesn't guarantee that mice will not risk their lives to seek food or shelter there. That's the life of a prey animal. The presence of a cat

will do nothing to deter mice if they have potential access to food and shelter. Remove the food and shelter, and the mice will go elsewhere.

## Why do some feral cats have the tips of their ears clipped off?

These are TNR cats, meaning trap, neuter, return. This is a tricky situation because the TNR cats have no other options. They are too feral to make good pets. Well-meaning people will trap these feral cats in order to have them neutered and vaccinated before releasing them back into the wild. While the veterinarian is performing the surgery, he will remove the tip of one of the cat's ears to ensure that the same cat is not trapped again.

This practice is well intentioned, but I still have a problem with it. Even though the cat can no longer reproduce, he can still do a great deal of damage to native wildlife. However, this really isn't a problem for feral cat colonies in inner city areas where there is no wildlife for them to decimate.

But no matter how much cat food is made available to feral cats, they still hunt. And if these TNR cats are maintained in areas where there is wildlife, they can

> **"CAT YEARS"**
> The average cat lives for eighteen years and is sexually mature by six months of age. So a six-month-old cat is the equivalent of a fourteen-year-old human. After the cat is six months old, each year is approximately equal to four human years.

do a lot of damage. For instance, here on Long Island, we have endangered birds such as piping plovers, and feral cats present a great risk for them. Many people tell me that the damage feral cats do to wildlife is greatly exaggerated. Or they say that it's no big deal if a cat eats a few mice or shrews. Maybe you see these animals as garden pests, but kestrels and owls rely on them to survive. So you can put up as many owl boxes as you want, but if there are no small native mammals for them to eat, you won't have any owls.

This is not the only issue that arises when maintaining colonies of feral cats. Once the general public becomes aware that people feed and care for these cats, they will begin dumping their unwanted cats into this population.

In a perfect world, TNR would be a great solution. But our world is not perfect.

## What's the difference between a stray cat and a feral cat?

A stray cat is a homeless cat that is equally comfortable wandering the streets or in the company of humans. A feral cat does not feel comfortable near humans. If trapped or confined with humans, he feels threatened and

compromised. Some feral cats can be rehabilitated to become good pets. I have successfully rehabilitated many, but not all, of the feral cats I've encountered.

I have had some trapped feral cats that were so wild at first that they would put mountain lions to shame. But once they were kept indoors in cages, they quickly became habituated to people. Ultimately, many of these cats turned out to be even needier and friendlier to humans than some cats that had been socialized at a very young age. Every cat is an individual, and rehabilitating feral cats is never a cut-and-dried issue.

I've heard that many cats live well into their twenties. What can I do to ensure that my cat lives a long life?

Some cats live well into their twenties, but I've personally never had a cat that lived past eighteen. And the major factors likely to compromise any cat's health are poor diet and accidental trauma like traffic accidents or encounters with wild animals. The best things you can do to guarantee a

long, healthy life for your cat is to keep him indoors, feed him the best possible diet, and take him for regular veterinary checkups. It's always better to be proactive than reactive.

## Can a cat overdose on catnip?

No. Catnip makes cats very, very happy, but it never actually enters the cat's bloodstream, so there is no way for it to enter the cat's brain. The cat's enjoyment of catnip is similar to the sensation you get from smelling a pleasant aroma like a fresh basil leaf. A cat can snap out of a catnip high any time he chooses to do so. Cats may behave as if it is a mind-altering hallucinogen, but catnip poses no danger to them.

## How many cats are too many?

That depends on the amount of money you have to give them proper food and veterinary care, the amount of time you have to keep them well groomed and keep their litter boxes clean, and the amount of space you have so they don't feel confined or compromised. It also depends on your friends and relatives.

If people don't want to come to your home because of the smell of the litter boxes, you either have too many cats or you are not caring for them properly. I've had up to eight cats in my house, and I have yet to have any guest come here and realize that eight cats live here. They never smell a litter box. There is no clawed furniture or shredded drapes.

Some cat owners have a blind spot about this, which is why cat hoarders don't realize they have too many cats. Having cats in your house does not mean that your house should be a mess as a result. Animal husbandry is all about keeping the animals comfortable in a pleasant environment. When we go to a zoo, we always expect the animals' habitats to look clean, comfortable, and attractive. We always judge a zoo based on the animals' living conditions. Our homes are the habitats for our pet animals, so visitors should perceive them as clean, presentable, and odor free. If your friends and relatives keep complaining, you should listen, because they may be right. And you may have too many cats.

## Thomas

We once had a very small Persian cat named Thomas. He was a very sickly kitten and weighed only 5 pounds at maturity. His health was never good. He had chronic diarrhea, bad gums, and a host of other medical issues, and to make matters worse, the other cats hated him. This wasn't limited to an occasional swat to chase him away from the food dish—they really hated him. And he was understandably afraid of them.

To maintain his quality of life, he spent all of his time in our bedroom, under the bed. The door was kept closed so the other cats could not come in and bother him. His food, water, and litter box were under the bed. He was so frightened of the other cats, and that was the only place in the house where he felt safe. He was just too small and frail to properly interact with other cats, so this is how he lived his life.

Every cat is different, and ultimately this was the best solution for Thomas.

## I want to get a kitten to keep my older cat company. What's the best way to ensure that they get along?

You can't ensure anything when it comes to cats and their relationships. I rarely see situations in which adult cats don't get along with, or at least tolerate, kittens. The best approach is to keep the kitten in a separate room with his own food, water, and litter pan, and keep the door closed. The adult and the kitten will sniff at each other under the door, and the adult will probably sit by the door with a bottle-brush tail and his fur puffed out, hurling abuse and insults at the kitten. After a couple of weeks, you will notice that the adult cat doesn't do this quite as much. Periodically carry the kitten around the house and show him to the other cat so that the two animals can get used to one another in a nonconfrontational setting.

When they finally do encounter each other, it's important to remember that cats communicate through snarls, hisses, and growls. Cats only meow to their mothers or to us. Two cats will never communicate with each other this way, but people can be upset by the snarls, growls, and hisses that make up normal cat communication. As a general rule, if two cats really don't like each other, you will know right away. The fighting will start immediately. If they are simply avoiding each other, that's fine. Of course, if one cat spends all of his time hiding under the bed, he needs a safe haven.

## I have a twelve-year-old cat and a four-year-old cat. On good days, they tolerate each other. On bad days, the younger one chases the older one around, trying to play with her, and she runs away hissing and growling. Is there anything I can do to make them better friends?

You say that there are good days and bad days, which means that there are days when everybody gets along. This is no different from human relationships.

Sometimes we get along, and sometimes we argue over the silliest things. If the only problem is chasing and growling, nothing bad is happening. There is no bloodshed, and neither cat is hiding all day. They are simply interacting in a way that is natural to social animals. If they eat out of the same bowl or sleep together, you have probably been witnessing nothing more serious than an argument. If both cats can eat, sleep, and use the litter box normally, what they do in between is their business.

## What is the best age to bring home a new kitten? Do you have any tips on how to choose a kitten with a good temperament?

I've brought home kittens that were only one hour old and still had the umbilical cord attached, and cats that were fifteen or sixteen years old. And they always seem to work pretty well in my household regardless of their age. In general, friendly kittens grow into friendly adults. But I have seen trapped feral kittens that hissed like wild banshees calm down and become friendly once they realized that no one was going to hurt them. So temperament is not something that you can really predict or guarantee.

The best way to make a choice is to ask advice of the breeder or the people in the shelter who are raising the litter. They can tell you which kittens are the most friendly and outgoing. Just ask them which kitten they would take home if they didn't already have ten or twelve (as most shelter workers already do).

As a general rule, kittens that remain with their siblings for the longest possible time adjust best to life as house pets. Kittens that are bottle raised and deprived of interaction with other cats tend to perceive humans as playthings. They have not had any opportunities to learn proper control during play with other kittens. Eight to nine weeks is a good age to bring home a new kitten. It is actually illegal to transport or sell kittens or puppies younger than eight weeks.

## Sometimes my cat comes up and nudges me to pet her. But after five or ten minutes of petting, she suddenly scratches me. What is wrong with her?

Cats are very tactile-oriented, and some cats are very sensitive to touch. If you pet them at the base of the tail or on the chin, they overreact. Many cats can't seem to get enough touching. But when you pet some cats for a long time, they can get so stimulated and aroused that they lose control and lash out. The cat really doesn't want to hurt you; he just can't help doing this.

Some cats bite, pant, or drool when they become overstimulated from too much petting. This is comparable to tickling a young child to the point where they are laughing so hard they lose all sense of reality. The key is to know how much intense petting your cat can tolerate before this happens and stop before he completely loses it. Or just don't pet him so hard—just a light tickle here and there. Every cat is different.

# What is the safest way to break up a fight between two cats?

It's a mistake to underestimate a cat's physical strength; very few adult men can successfully restrain a panicked cat.

Stay far away and throw a big coat or blanket over them. Once they are in the dark, they will panic, let go, and run in opposite directions. Keep your hands far away. Cat bites can easily put you in the hospital. A cat's claws and teeth are covered with bacteria, and a puncture wound is like an injection of toxins. I've had my share of infections from cat bites and scratches. It's much easier to have your cat treated at the vet than to end up in the hospital yourself. And who will take the cat to the vet if you are in the hospital because you got all scratched up when stopping the fight?

# I adopted a special-needs cat from the shelter. I was told that he was a feral cat. I am having a lot of trouble socializing him. How long does this normally take?

This depends on what the cat was exposed to in the past. My preferred method to socialize a feral cat is to force him to be in contact with people by keeping them in a large cage in the busiest room of the house. If you simply allow the cat to run away and hide, he will never have the opportunity to learn that people pose no threat. He may have had negative experiences with people in the past, but it's not going to happen in the future. Only regular positive interactions with people will help the cat change his mind about this, and only the cat can make this decision.

Obviously, you can't simply grab the cat and force him to interact with people, so a large cat cage is the easiest. These cages are made by the same companies that make dog crates. They usually measure 2 feet wide, 4 feet tall, and 3 feet long. Put a bed and a litter pan in the bottom of the cage, and set it up in the busiest room of your house. Most likely, the cat will just hide in the litter box for the first four or five days. But as the world goes past his cage and no harm comes to him, he will gradually realize that he is safe. Once the cat

starts to look relaxed and calm and he carries his tail up, then you know it's time to let him loose in the house. The cat might not be ready to voluntarily jump into someone's lap or tolerate being picked up. Every cat is different and some will require more time to become well socialized. But keeping him in a high-traffic area of your home is the best way to teach him that humans pose no threat.

Just consider all of the things that cats have acclimated themselves to over the ages. Cats have lived in deserts, in pyramids, in forests, and on busy city streets. They also learned that running and hiding was a good way to prolong their lives. Once a cat becomes a house pet, the need to run away and hide is no longer important to his well-being, but it's up to the cat to make this determination.

## My kitten was so playful when she was a baby. But as she gets older, she seems to want less and less to do with me. Why?

Every baby grows up. Some cats retain their kittenlike ways as they get older, but many do not. If your mature cat no longer chooses to act like a kitten, your best solution is to get another kitten. As that kitten matures, he will be good company for the first cat. When he grows up, you can get another kitten. This system works great as long as you don't acquire more cats than you can afford to keep properly.

## I adopted two kittens when they were six weeks old. They got along great until they were about a year old. Now they don't seem to like each other at all. What do I do?

You don't have to like everyone that you work or live with. The fact that the two cats are cohabiting and going about their daily routine without compromising each other's welfare enhances their quality of life regardless of their interactions. Some cats that live together are very affectionate with one another. They play together, groom one another, and sleep together. Many cats are not like this. As long as one cat is not living in constant fear, hiding under the bed, or afraid to eat or use the litter box, this is not something you need to worry about. Both cats will still have a very good quality of life, including the pleasure of having another cat around to talk to. Just imagine how lonely you would feel if you were stranded on a desert island with no one to talk to. If there was another person there, even if you didn't particularly like him, you would be happy to have someone you could relate to. Pets are the same. They appreciate the company of their own species even if they don't always show it.

## My two cats were best friends for years. The older one died a few months ago, and I didn't want the other one to be lonely, so I got a kitten. But the kitten is afraid of my older cat. How can I help?

The kitten is afraid because he is a little kitten and the other one is an old cranky cat. But even if they don't like each other now, the kitten will lose his fear as he grows up. And the fact that there is another cat in the house will enhance your older cat's quality of life. It will get his mind off his former routine and the loss of his companion. As long as the older cat is not

### MALE-ORDER PETS
I've had male and female cats my whole life, but my favorites have always been males. I can't say if this is just a coincidence, but the closest relationships I have had with cats, including wild cats I kept in captivity, have always been with males. There is no scientific reason for this. I really can't explain it. Oddly, my favorite dogs, birds, and rabbits have also been males.

## Cats and Babies

When my wife was pregnant with my son, we had eight cats and one North American bobcat living in the house, plus assorted ravens, cockatoos, dogs, snakes, lizards, and many other animals. Neither my wife's family nor mine were animal lovers. They all envisioned my poor baby suffering a dire fate at the hands of all of these animals. My wife's side of the family was mainly concerned about her contracting toxoplasmosis from the kitty litter boxes.

My side of the family was thoroughly convinced that a cat would get into the nursery and suffocate the baby by sucking his breath away. I distinctly remember my father getting rid of my pet cat when my little sister was born. He found the cat in my baby sister's room and feared it would suck her breath out. This old myth most likely came about before crib death was understood. Every now and then, some poor unfortunate child died of crib death and the cat was blamed. Perhaps the cat was found in the baby's crib because that was the warmest spot in the house, or maybe it was just human nature to blame cats for everything.

Since there was no reasoning with my superstitious family, the only way to keep peace was to put a screen door on the baby's room. This way, we could see and hear the baby, but animals could not get in there. My son is now ten. He obviously survived a childhood with cats, and I am still on speaking terms with my family thanks to a $49.95 screen door from The Home Depot. Sometimes compromise is the best way to go.

physically harming the kitten, this should be a temporary problem. The kitten will decide that there is no reason to fear the older cat.

**I have had one cat for four years, and we've both been pretty happy. Recently, friends have urged me to get a second cat, insisting that Mookie must be lonely during the day when I'm at work. I think she's fine on her own. What should I do?**

Your cat probably is lonely when you are at work, and she probably would like to have another cat around for company. However, your cat doesn't know that living with another cat is an option. Animals live in the moment, so Mookie is not sitting there all day, looking out the window, wishing there were another cat in the house. She is content in her own little world. If you did bring another cat into the house, it would probably cause some temporary confusion at first. But Mookie's life would be better in the long run because she would have another cat to relate to.

However, don't do this unless you want to have two cats and you can afford two cats. If you don't want to clean two litter boxes, take two cats to the vet every year, and buy twice as much cat food, don't get another cat no matter what your friends say. Your cat isn't wishing for another cat; your friends are. And they probably don't want to come over and clean out the litter boxes for you.

## My kitten seems very aggressive. Will she outgrow this?

Most likely, you are misinterpreting play behavior as true aggression. A kitten that bounds after you, snatches at your feet, and jumps on you is really not being aggressive. She is trying to play. Since there are no other kittens around, she will play with you that way. If you respond by pushing her away, scolding her, or otherwise interacting, she will see this as encouragement to continue doing it.

The sock toy I recommended earlier in the book is the perfect remedy in this situation. The idea is to redirect the kitten's play behavior from you to the sock toy. Let the kitten pounce on it, grab it, and expend her playfulness on something other than your skin.

If your cat were truly aggressive, you would end up in the hospital, which has happened to me many times.

## One of my cats likes to attack the other while he's sleeping. How do I get him to stop?

You can't make a cat do anything. Only the other cat can stop this behavior. Some cats are more tolerant, and if cat A insists on waking cat B in this rough manner and cat B accepts it, cat B really doesn't mind. So you should probably stay out of it. If one cat is really bothering the other one, you are going to know it. The cat will start hiding under the bed; he won't come out to eat. In other words, his life will be truly compromised. But an occasional disagreement between cats really doesn't fall into this category.

In human society, we have arguments all the time. In the heat of the moment, you may say or do horrible things. Later, when your blood cools

down, your next statement might be, "Where should we go for dinner?" Things like this happen in any normal social relationship, and cats are the same. Two cats may have a terrible argument, but a couple of hours later you will find them sleeping together or eating from the same bowl.

## What's a good cat breed to have around children?

Cats have been domesticated for a fairly short time, and most of the cat breeds today have only existed since the 1950s or later. In contrast to domesticated dogs, cats haven't really been bred to fulfill any specific purpose. Therefore, one breed of cat cannot be described as better adapted to the role of a companion, although there are certain dog breeds that are considered primarily companion breeds.

Dogs have been domesticated for 20,000 years and in that time we have altered their behavior as well as their appearance. We have created different cat breeds by altering the way they look, but we have not made any changes to the way they think. Most distinct cat breeds began as random spontaneous

mutations. These caused variations in coat color or length, ear carriage, muzzle length, tail length, body proportions—but none of these changes was linked to a specific working function. All breeds of cat perceive and respond to the world in the same way.

If you want to find a good cat for your child, take him or her to the animal shelter to see the available cats. Look for cats that appear calm but sociable—not fearful or aggressive. And ask the shelter workers which ones they would consider best suited to a role as a youngster's companion.

## Are there any cat breeds known to get along well with dogs?

Cats all view the world the same way, but this is not true for dogs. A breed that was designed to hunt, such as one of the coonhounds, and a breed that was genetically selected to be a companion, such as a Bichon, may perceive a small kitten in very different ways. However, all cats respond to threats in the same way—either fight or run. And every breed of cat from Sphynx to Persian will respond in one of these ways if it perceives a dog as a threat.

However, cats may view dogs differently on an individual basis. I've never seen any cat that was incapable of changing his mind about dogs when he realized that dogs posed no danger to him.